Cajun Foodways

CAJUN
FOODWAYS

C. Paige Gutierrez

UNIVERSITY PRESS OF MISSISSIPPI
JACKSON AND LONDON

Photographs by Jay Elledge, Philip Gould, and Ginette Vachon are courtesy of the Center for Acadian and Creole Folklore at the University of Southwestern Louisiana. All other photographs are courtesy of Barry Jean Ancelet.

Manufactured in the United States of America
Designed by Sally Hamlin
Print on Demand Edition
95 94 93 92   4 3 2 1

The paper in this book meets the guidelines for permanence and durability of the Committee on Production Guidelines for Book Longevity of the Council on Library Resources.

Library of Congress Cataloging-in-Publication Data

Gutierrez, C. Paige.
  Cajun foodways / C. Paige Gutierrez.
    p. cm.
  Includes bibliographical references and index.
  ISBN 0-87805-562-2 (cloth : alk. paper). — ISBN 0-87805-563-0
(paper : alk. paper)
    1. Cajuns—Folklore. 2. Food habits—Louisiana. 3. Cookery,
Cajun. 4. Cajuns—Social life and customs. 5. Louisiana—Social
life and customs. I. Title.
GR111.F73G85 1992
394.1'2'089410763—dc20   92-9963
                                                                     CIP

British Library Cataloging-in-Publication data available

Contents

Foreword

During the 1980s, bigger-than-life chef Paul Prudhomme brought his native Cajun cooking to the attention of the nation by appearing on national television and cooking for heads of state and media celebrities. The excitement generated by his enthusiasm and spicy seasonings brought Cajun culture and its cuisine to the attention of the nation, fueling a fad which swept through restaurants across the country. Unfortunately, fads are usually based on trendy fascination instead of deep understanding, and many came to know only a caricature of Cajun cooking. Chefs everywhere copied Prudhomme's blackened redfish, and eventually blackened just about everything else. Cayenne peppers began to appear everywhere, including Prudhomme's Cajun martinis and "Original Cajun Flavored Beer" (brewed "in the time-honored Cajun tradition," in Milwaukee, Wisconsin.)

Here in south Louisiana, many people have become self-conscious about the new popularity of things Cajun. Efforts to improve connotation of the word Cajun date back only to the late 1960s. Before that, Cajun in English usually referred to the poor, white, French-speaking underclass. Yet by the 1970s, the sports teams of the University of Southwestern Louisiana were called the Ragin' Cajuns. Soon after, many restaurant owners began including the all-important new key word in their messages, including Enola Prudhomme's Cajun Cafe, Lagneaux's Cajun Style Buffet, Prejean's Comfortable Cajun Dining, Don's Seafood Hut Serves a Good Cajun Meal, Blair House Traditional and Progressive Cajun Cuisine, Randol's Restaurant and Cajun Dance Hall, and, of course, Mulate's, the World's Most Famous Cajun Restaurant.

This burst of ethnic pride coincided with the appearance of the word

Cajun on just about every commodity remotely associated with Louisiana French culture: one can now go fishing in a Cajun brand bass boat, using Cajun brand crickets for bait, keeping Cajun brand beer on Cajun brand ice in a Cajun brand cooler, and cook the catch later in a "Cajun microwave" (actually, a moist-heat smoker). A local portable toilet company calls itself K-Jon. It's almost as though we have been afraid of forgetting who we are. When local musician, accordion builder and sage, Marc Savoy, was asked recently, "Aren't you sorry the Cajuns have been discovered?", he answered, "I'm even sorrier the Cajuns have discovered themselves," and went on to predict that Cajun society was in danger of dying of "acute cuteness."

On the other hand, there has been an explosion of creativity in Cajun cooking. Beginning as far back as the turn of this century, newspaper recipes and new commodities such as stoves and refrigerators made new ingredients and new techniques available to housewives who were increasingly freed from outdoor farm duties to concentrate their efforts in their kitchens. Restaurant chefs experimented with the bounty of seafood available and introduced such delicacies as Oysters Rockefeller and Crabmeat au gratin to the local population. Crawfish, so closely associated now with Cajun identity, have not been widely eaten until recently. As late as the 1930s, a USDA agent complained in a letter to his superiors that crawfish were plentiful and would be an excellent source of protein for poor Cajuns but that he could not convince them to eat the crawfish more frequently. A dish as seemingly definitive as crawfish etouffee only appeared as late as the 1950s when a few entrepreneurs first made peeled crawfish tails commercially available. Since then crawfish tails have found their way into surprising new dishes. Today, there are crawfish egg rolls, crawfish enchiladas, and crawfish fettucini. Housewives and restaurant chefs continued to experiment with new Cajun foods, keeping the Cajun tradition not only alive, but ever changing. My own mother has developed a wonderful casserole with crawfish, Swiss Gruyere cheese, butter, cream, and mushrooms.

Yet the Cajuns' now-celebrated cuisine was once a source of embarrassment and self-deprecating humor:

Q: Do you know the difference between an ordinary zoo and a Cajun zoo?

A: A Cajun zoo has a recipe next to the name of the animal on each cage.

And, this example:

Q: Do you know what a Cajun seven-course meal is?

A: A pound of boudin and a six-pack.

But with the fad, Cajun music joined Cajun cooking as a rallying point for ethnic pride. A few years ago, a rash of bumper stickers boldly declared that "Cajuns make better lovers because they eat anything." Crawfish have become a cultural symbol, as afficionados sport T-shirts with a cryptic (and suggestive) version of the directions for eating boiled crawfish: "Pinch my tail, suck my head." A new wave of telegenic Cajun chefs, such as Paul Prudhomme, Alex Patout and John Folse, seem to be undoing some of the media damage caused by years of parodies by such comedians as Cajun chef Justin Wilson. Even McDonald's marketed a Cajun McChicken sandwich and Cajun Fries. So I was somewhat surprised recently when a friend showed me an article in *The New York Times* entitled "Cajun Cooking is Dead." So, that was it. Ah, well, easy come, easy go. Live by the fad, die by the fad. Cajun cooking was dead and we didn't even know it here in south Louisiana. I didn't know how I would break the news to my mother. I read on and learned that the article under this presumptuous little title was actually a food critic's review of the temporary branch of K-Paul's Louisiana Kitchen in the trendy city. What the critic meant was that his interest in Cajun cooking, specifically Paul Prudhomme's version, was dead, along with the interest of most of his hyper-hip readers who depend on such reviews to know where they're not supposed to be seen eating that week. I was relieved. I went home and had a bowl of gumbo to celebrate. Mama laughed.

Despite the critic's gloomy pronouncement, Cajun cooking has been recognized as one of America's regional culinary styles and what are perceived as Cajun dishes now adorn menus in many restaurants across the country. Despite the popularity of Cajun food, most Americans still know little about the culture behind the menu entries. French anthropologist Claude Levi-Strauss made it abundantly clear in *The Raw and the Cooked* that there is an important relationship between people and the food they eat. In this book, C. Paige Gutierrez applies the principals of anthropological foodways research to her study of Cajun culture of south

Louisiana. Her analysis races past the surface hype to get at the substructure of the issues. This book happens to be about the Cajuns of south Louisiana, who don't eat to live but live to eat, but it's more important than that. This is a fascinating exploration of the relationship between what, where, and how we eat and who we are—the cultural and ethnic definitions to be found on the plates on all our tables.

Barry Jean Ancelet

Preface

This book is about the relationship between Cajun food and Cajun ethnic identity. It is not a cookbook, or a nutritional study, or a history of Cajuns or of their food. Rather, it is a description and interpretation of the symbolic aspects of Cajun ethnic foodways, based on field research in Louisiana and written from the perspective of folklore studies and cultural anthropology.

Scholars in these fields use the term *foodways* to refer not only to food and cooking but to all food-related activities, concepts, and beliefs shared by a particular group of people. Many scholars who have studied foodways say that food has a symbolic or expressive dimension, that it conveys meaning. My purpose here is to explore how foodways convey meaning for a particular ethnic group, and to interpret the nature of the messages expressed regarding ethnic identity.

Folklorists, by definition, have an interest in traditional culture—those customs, values, and ways of seeing the world that typify life in a particular community. Traditional culture is passed down from generation to generation, usually orally or by direct demonstration, and it is often rooted in a particular natural environment. Foreign to, and often at odds with, traditional or folk culture are mass media, mass marketing, and mass bureaucracies, all of which pressure people to conform to a modern, centralized, standardized lifestyle and worldview—a now global process which Alan Lomax describes as cultural "grey-out" (Lomax 1977).

Ethnic and regional groups throughout the world face the double tug of the traditional and the modern. Why do people in the modern world, such as Cajuns and other ethnic groups, celebrate their traditions? Cajuns' attention to their own traditional foodways is more than merely nostalgia, or a clever marketing ploy to lure tourists and sell local products. The symbolic power of Cajun food is deeply rooted in Cajuns' relationships with their natural environment and with other people, both Cajuns and non-Cajuns.

The idea for this study of Cajun food and ethnic identity was inspired by Cajuns themselves. Before beginning field research in Louisiana, I made two preliminary trips to the state in 1978, to Bayou Lafourche in southeastern Louisiana and to the Lafayette area in the southwestern part of the state. As an anthropologist and folklorist specializing in the American South, I was curious about this group of southerners who deviate in important ways from the usual definitions of southerners. I was also curious about what was happening to traditional Cajun culture and identity in the midst of a then booming, oil-based economy; a large influx of non-Cajun newcomers; and general participation in modern American life.

These interests coalesced with the decision to focus on foodways and their relationship to contemporary Cajun identity. This decision grew out of observations I made during my preliminary field trips: the people I met spent a great deal of time cooking, eating, talking about food, and bragging about how special Cajun food is. This was the case seven years before Cajun food became the focus of intense national media attention in the mid-1980s.

Some societies place more emphasis on their foodways than do others; they are more "preoccupied" with food and cooking than are other societies (Chang 1977:12). Cajuns claim to be unusually food-oriented, especially talented in food preparation, and distinctive in their ability to enjoy food. In addition, foods are frequently used as ethnic and regional emblems in Cajun Louisiana, a trend in keeping with the self-proclaimed concern with foods.

I gathered much of the field data used in this study in the town of Breaux Bridge (St. Martin Parish) during a ten-month period in 1979–80. I conducted research in the city of Lafayette (Lafayette Parish) for three months in late 1978 and continued to gather data there while I was living in nearby Breaux Bridge. From 1980 to 1983 I lived in Baton Rouge, where I collected data from the many Cajuns who are temporary or permanent residents of this border city to Acadiana. I also made numerous short field trips to communities throughout south Louisiana during my residency in the state.

The city of Lafayette is located in the eastern portion of southwestern Louisiana's prairie country, about fifteen miles west of the edge of the Atchafalaya Basin swamp. It grew out of the consolidation of several primarily Acadian settlements on the Vermilion River. During antebellum days, the area served as a market and service center for the many small plantations surrounding it. Lafayette's role as a regional "hub city" strengthened in the late nineteenth century with the building of the Southern Pacific Railroad through the town and was assured with the founding in 1900 of the college that later became the University of Southwestern Louisiana. Because Lafayette has long been a commercial, service, and educational center, its middle-class population is proportionately larger than that of most Cajun towns, and its citizens' espousal of "progressive" values can be traced to antebellum times (see Dismukes 1972).

Lafayette is the administrative center of the south Louisiana oil industry. In the 1970s and early 1980s Lafayette residents referred to their town as a small Houston because of its wealth, rapid growth, and crippling traffic jams. During that period, when the oil industry was booming, some analysts claimed that Lafayette had a higher percentage of millionaires than any other U.S. city of its size, while others pointed out that "more distinctive if less dramatic is the fact that affluence is spread throughout much of the population" (Edmunds 1981). Lafayette is the birthplace of what some have called the "French Renaissance movement"—an effort to preserve French language and culture in Louisiana. The city is a center for activities related to the display of Cajun ethnic heritage and pride.

Breaux Bridge is a small Cajun and Afro-French town, located six miles east of the expanding fringes of Lafayette in predominantly rural St. Martin Parish. The settlement that later became known as Breaux Bridge was founded on the banks of Bayou Teche by Acadian refugees in 1766. The immediate area was populated by small farmers. The settlement slowly grew into a local trade and market center during the nineteenth century because of the bridge built across Bayou Teche by the Breaux family (Rees 1976). Today Breaux Bridge is still a market, service, and mercantile center for St. Martin Parish, with commercial and residential areas on both sides of the bayou. During the 1970s Interstate

10 was completed through south Louisiana, with an exit at Breaux Bridge.

To the east of Breaux Bridge is the Atchafalaya Basin swamp, the region's major source of wild crawfish and other swamp products. To the south in the sugar plantation country of Bayou Teche is St. Martinville, the oldest Acadian settlement in southwestern Louisiana and also a major center of white French Creole culture. To the north and west of Breaux Bridge are prairie country, the Anse La Butte oil field (one of the oldest in south Louisiana), and the city of Lafayette. All are within fifteen miles of Breaux Bridge, and all have influenced the town's social, cultural, and economic history.

A historical marker in Breaux Bridge reads as follows: "Breaux Bridge: Founded 1859. Long recognized for its culinary artistry in the preparation of crawfish. The 1958 Louisiana Legislature officially designated Breaux Bridge 'La Capitale Mondiale De L'ecrevisse' in honor of its centennial year." Breaux Bridge was known for its restaurants as early as the 1920s, and since 1960 it has been famous for its Crawfish Festival, now a biennial event that draws as many as 100,000 locals and tourists to the town for a three-day weekend in late spring. The festival has made Breaux Bridge locally and nationally known as a center of Cajun cuisine and Cajun joie de vivre (Trillin 1974).

The generalizations made in this study, especially those pertaining to descriptions of food types, best apply to the Breaux Bridge/Lafayette area of Acadiana. However, whenever possible I have cross-checked my Breaux Bridge/Lafayette data with data from other locations, as well as with the conclusions of other researchers in various parts of south Louisiana. This cross-checking has prompted me to make certain generalizations about the entire region or sections of the region.

The introductory chapter of this book presents an overview of Cajun history and a discussion of contemporary Cajun ethnic identity. Chapters 1, 2, and 3 provide general descriptions of Cajun food and cooking. Chapters 4, 5, and 6 focus on the crawfish as food and as symbol. Chapters 7 and 8 apply the insights gained through the analysis of crawfish to additional Cajun foodways.

Some of the ideas presented in the chapters on crawfish foodways appeared in seminal form in *Ethnic and Regional Foodways in the United States: The Performance of Group Identity*, edited by Linda Keller Brown and Kay Mussell. (Copyright © 1984 by The University of Tennessee Press. Used by permission.)

I wish to thank the many people in south Louisiana who helped me learn about Cajun food firsthand, especially those who live in the town of Breaux Bridge, where I did most of my field work.

CAJUN FOODWAYS

INTRODUCTION

Louisiana's Cajuns

During the 1980s Cajun food was a favorite topic of food critics and travel writers. Countless magazine and newspaper articles featured Cajun cooking, and restaurants in New York, Los Angeles, and other cities far from south Louisiana's Cajun country served Cajun-style food to eager customers. Cajun cooking was the subject of television talk shows, cooking classes, mail-order catalogs, specialty food shops, cookbooks, and how-to video tapes. New "gourmet" food products, such as frozen Cajun entrees and prepared Cajun seasoning powders, appeared on supermarket shelves. Cajun food became firmly established as an ethnic cuisine, far from its Louisiana homeland. Today Americans order dishes called "Cajun" from the menus of elegant restaurants, family-style eateries, and fast-food outlets. The nationwide popularity of Cajun food continues to grow, despite announcements by food critics in New York and California that Cajun cooking is no longer in fashion (Bourg 1985; Cutler 1989). Cajun food has become a product that can be marketed successfully to consumers outside Louisiana. But for Cajuns, this food is much more than a marketable product or a national fad: it is important for reasons beyond its enticing flavors and nutritional value.

By eating (or not eating) certain foods, people make a statement about their ethnic affiliation. But are such foodways merely indicators of eth-

3

nic identity, or do they also say something about the nature of that identity, about the values and self-image held by members of a group? How do foods and foodways convey such meanings? This book explores the answers to these questions in terms of Cajuns and their food, illustrating a basic tenet of the study of foodways: that food and identity are interconnected symbolically, and that each aids in the understanding of the other (see Brown and Mussell 1984; Farb and Armelagos 1980). Beginning with an overview of Cajun history and a discussion of contemporary Cajun identity, this study provides a description of Cajun foodways and an interpretation of the symbolic aspects of foodways and their role in the expression of ethnic identity.

ACADIANA, PAST AND PRESENT

Louisiana has two distinct parts, north and south. North Louisiana includes the northern half of the state and most of the territory of the "Florida" parishes (counties) north of Lake Pontchartrain and east of the Mississippi River. It is populated largely by Anglo-American and Afro-American Protestants. North Louisiana has more in common geographically, historically, and culturally with neighboring areas of Mississippi, Arkansas, and Texas than with south Louisiana, and it is readily categorized as part of the larger region of the American South.

South Louisiana encompasses the twenty-two parishes in the predominantly Cajun and Afro-French area known as Acadiana, as well as the city of New Orleans, the rim of Lake Pontchartrain, and the Mississippi River delta parishes in extreme southeastern Louisiana. Largely Catholic, south Louisiana is ethnically diverse, although French influence (continental, Acadian, and/or Caribbean) was predominant throughout the colonial era and remains strong in Acadiana. South Louisiana is not typical of the American South; rather, it is in many ways a distinct region that lies south of the South.

The physical geography of south Louisiana is unusual compared to that of other regions of the American South. The natural terrain includes four basic types: the prairies of southwestern Louisiana, subdivided into large sections by tree-lined bayous; the marshes of the coastal regions; the relatively elevated and extremely fertile natural levee lands found along the rivers and major bayous; and the swamps located behind the levee lands or elsewhere, including the 500,000-acre Atchafalaya Basin swamp, which separates southeastern from southwestern Louisiana. The numerous bayous, rivers, and lakes of the interior, plus 1,500 miles of meandering coastline, have served as avenues of transportation since precolonial times. The warm, humid, semitropical climate allows for long growing seasons, and serious droughts are rare. These physical and climatic factors have made it possible for south Louisiana to become a major producer of sugar, rice, cotton, corn, soybeans, cattle, oysters, shrimp, crabs, finfish, wildfowl, fur, and lumber, as well as items less prominent in the national economy, such as perique tobacco, Easter lilies, peppers, Spanish moss, crawfish, frogs, and alligator meat and hides. Abundant oil, gas, sulfur, salt, and other mineral reserves are part of the natural wealth of the region.

South Louisiana enjoys great cultural diversity. The population of the region today includes descendants of many cultural groups: Native Americans; various peoples of French extraction (continental French, Acadian French, non-Acadian Canadian French, Caribbean French Creoles); African, Afro-Caribbean, and Afro-American slaves; free persons of color originating both from within Louisiana and from Haiti; Germans and Swiss; Canary Islanders (Islenos) and continental Spanish; Cubans, Mexicans, and various Latin Americans; British, Irish, and Scots people; Italians, Sicilians, Greeks, and Croatians; Lebanese; Jews; Filipinos; Chinese; tidewater and upland southerners; upper Mississippi and Ohio Valley frontiersmen; and midwesterners. More recent immigrants include Vietnamese, Laotian, and Haitian refugees; oil workers from Texas and elsewhere; and, during the economic boom of the 1970s and early 1980s, job-seekers from the Snow Belt (called Michiganders). Despite this diversity, a Louisiana brand of French culture held sway throughout colonial times, and the Americanization that began after the Louisiana Purchase in 1803 had little influence in some areas until well into the twentieth century. This is particularly true of Acadiana, the land settled by the Acadian refugees and still dominated by their descendants, the Cajuns.

This study is primarily concerned with Acadiana, although at times the focus widens to include all of south Louisiana. Perhaps because Acadiana is the largest subregion of south Louisiana, or perhaps because of the many environmental and cultural similarities between Acadiana and the rest of south Louisiana, many people use the terms *Acadiana, Cajun country, south Louisiana,* and *French Louisiana* synonymously. Technically, however, the last two terms are more inclusive in that they include urban New Orleans and neighboring rural areas as well as Acadiana. New Orleans is not a Cajun city, even though Cajun culture is now marketed to tourists as one of many reasons to visit the city. Although Acadiana and south Louisiana seem similar when contrasted with Anglo-America at large, their differences are apparent from a local perspective. A diverse though predominantly French Catholic heritage and similar physical environments unite Acadiana to the rest of south Louisiana, but the local dominance of the more specifically Cajun heritage distinguishes Acadiana from the larger region. The 1968 Louisiana state legislature implicitly recognized these facts when it designated a twenty-two-parish area of south Louisiana as "Acadiana"—a name derived from the words *Acadian* and *Louisiana*.

The French who settled in what is now Nova Scotia in the seventeenth century became known there as Acadians. They prospered in Canada until 1755, when the British seized their holdings and ousted them from Acadia. After years of hardship, rejection, and wandering, many Acadian refugees settled permanently in southern Louisiana. Their life in frontier Louisiana required adjustment to a physical environment that included bayous, swamps, marshes, and prairies, and adaptation to a social environment that commingled peoples of many origins in an evolving New World cultural mix. The settlers whose families already had lived for several generations in Louisiana when the Acadians arrived called themselves Creole, meaning "native" or "local."[1] The Acadian settlers adopted

---

1. This is only one of many meanings for the word *Creole*, or *creole*, in Louisiana. The word may be used as a noun or an adjective; its meaning varies according to historical period, geographic area, identity of users, context of use, and the speaker's degree of knowledge of the ethnographic situation. In Louisiana the word originally meant "native" as a noun or adjective and was used to distinguish people, animals, and products that were born or originated in the colony as opposed to the mother country. *Creole* has since been used with various referents, including but not limited to the following: the descendants of the original French and Spanish settlers; the wealthy descendants of these settlers; the descendants of the offspring of French and blacks; any persons of partial African descent; any black or partially black person of French culture and language. In addition, the word is frequently used today to refer to any person or thing of or from New Orleans, or any person or thing of or from south Louisiana (including Cajuns). These usages are common among outsiders and others with little knowledge of the word's ethnographic and historic referents. *Creole*

much from Creole culture in Louisiana, yet maintained their own identity in the process. During the nineteenth century, the word *Acadian* became *Cajun*, a term used to describe a new American ethnic group that had emerged as the dominant cultural group—and the most numerous element of the population—in much of rural south Louisiana (see Ancelet, Edwards, and Pitre [1991:36–38]; Dorman [1983]).

The Cajuns' ancestors were rural, French-speaking Catholics who made their new homes in a setting that was also largely rural, French-speaking, and Catholic. Thus, they experienced much less pressure to change in these broad respects, than they would have if they had settled in the British seaboard colonies. The few Acadians who were upwardly mobile often affiliated with the French Creole elite or, less frequently, with the fast-rising Americans who entered south Louisiana after the Louisiana Purchase. But most Acadians and their descendants, particularly those who lived in isolated areas as small farmers, ranchers, fishermen, trappers, and hunters maintained a traditional or folk lifestyle—although the exact nature of that lifestyle varied with the environment. Like many other folk groups, these Acadians led lives centered on family and community; they participated very little in the political and educational institutions of the larger society. They usually married other members of their own group, but occasionally married non-Acadian white settlers, often of French, German, Spanish, or Anglo-American origin. The children usually were raised as Acadian. Geographic isolation, illiteracy, and language barriers shielded them in varying degrees from the modern or mainstream culture of the day, and they retained traditional styles of architecture, foods, crafts, music, and other forms of entertainment.

When mainstream America came to Acadiana in the twentieth century in the form of forced English-language education, modern highways, the

---

also may refer to the French Creole language, which is found in the French Caribbean, Louisiana, and elsewhere. It is also sometimes used, less precisely, to refer to any kind of Louisiana French language. Given the many meanings of *Creole* in Louisiana, it is not surprising that the word often causes confusion and argument among locals, including those who may refer to themselves as Creole. Although a speaker's definition of the word may often be inferred from context, the listener sometimes has no recourse other than to ask, "What do you mean by *Creole?*" For further information on the use of the term in Louisiana, see Dominguez (1977) and Spitzer (1986).

mass media, the petrochemical industry, and World War II, Cajuns found themselves in a position not unlike that of newly arrived Old World immigrants to the United States. Although this new world of the outsider offered many opportunities for a better life, it also threatened to destroy much that was traditional and meaningful in the old way of life. Local customs were often ridiculed by the more "sophisticated" Anglo-American newcomers, and the use of the French language in public schools was forbidden by state law. American business and industry rewarded formal educational skills and a proficiency in standard English which, initially, few Cajuns possessed. Many outsiders—and insiders as well—associated Cajun culture with ignorance and poverty. Following in the footsteps of their nineteenth-century predecessors, twentieth-century observers continued to stereotype Cajuns as either virtuous peasants living in an idyllic, romanticized setting, or as mysterious, violent, hedonistic swamp dwellers (Conrad 1983; Dorman 1983).

Compulsory English education, the pervasive mass media, the influx of English-speaking outsiders, and the recognition by Cajuns of the social and economic advantages of speaking English led to the almost total elimination of the French language among the younger generation by the 1950s. The parents of these children had been punished in school for speaking French—their only language—and they had been ridiculed all their lives for their nonstandard variety of French or their accented English. They had learned to be ashamed of their language and of Cajun culture in general. Like the Anglo-American outsiders and the Acadian and white Creole elite, they came to associate the speaking of Cajun French with ignorance and poverty. Cajuns of the 1930s, 1940s, and early 1950s bore the brunt of the sometimes painful transition from a traditional, French-speaking society to a modern, English-speaking one, and Cajun self-esteem was low during those years. In an effort to spare their children the social humiliation and economic disadvantages they themselves had experienced, they raised their children to conform to national norms in language and culture. Their success in doing so has had a surprising, unintended effect. These Americanized children came of age at a time when people around the country were rediscovering their roots. Interest in ethnicity was a national trend. Cajuns, especially the younger generations, were sufficiently Americanized to be well aware of national trends, and they recognized the local implications of the value of ethnicity discovered by other groups. During the 1960s and 1970s Cajun self-confidence and identity strengthened, at the same time as both local and outside interest in Cajun culture was growing. Cajun identity in both its traditional and modern aspects became a source of pride.

The revival of Cajun ethnic pride has been fostered in part by the efforts of what some have called the "French Renaissance" movement, a collection of organizations concerned with the preservation and promotion of French language and culture in Louisiana. Preeminent among these organizations is the Council for the Development of French in Louisiana, called CODOFIL, a semi-independent state agency created by the legislature in 1968. James Domengeaux, a Lafayette lawyer and politician, was the driving force behind CODOFIL until his death in 1988. CODOFIL has urged Cajuns and others to speak French and to pass the language on to their children. The agency has worked to preserve the French language and identity in the state through language education programs, heritage festivals, French-language media, and cultural exchange programs between Louisiana and other parts of the French-speaking world.

CODOFIL has tried to instill in outsiders, including the national media, a knowledge of and respect for the Louisiana French heritage. Auxiliary to both of these goals has been the refutation of negative stereotypes concerning Cajuns. CODOFIL's efforts have resulted in an increase in positive media coverage of Cajun Louisiana at the local, national, and international levels since the late 1960s. The agency has also encouraged tourism and outside investments, leading to an influx of sympathetic and interested tourists and investors, both American and foreign, especially French, Canadian, and Belgian. In addition, heritage festivals cosponsored by CODOFIL have been very successful in highlighting various aspects of traditional culture, including Cajun music, dance, food, and crafts (Dorman 1983).

As Louisiana's largest French-speaking group, Cajuns have been a major focus of and primary participants in the French Renaissance movement and its programs. Although the French Renaissance movement has undoubtedly been instrumental in strengthening pride in the Cajun heritage, it has not been without its local critics. Some have asserted that CODOFIL's emphasis on teaching and promoting standard French is inappropriate for Cajuns, who often speak nonstandard French or no

French at all. For some Cajuns, the CODOFIL philosophy—a reflection of the concerns of the organization's relatively wealthy and educated leadership—is a reminder of the age-old uneasiness between the "average" Cajuns and the Acadian and white Creole elite (Dorman 1983). Cajuns' responses to CODOFIL and the French Renaissance movement have varied, with some Cajuns participating fully, some showing little or no interest, some vocally opposing the movement, and some attempting to change its direction.

In addition to CODOFIL, various public and private institutions and individuals have played a role in the revival of Cajun pride. For example, regional media provide a significant forum for the expression of Cajun identity. In the past twenty years, Cajuns have increasingly produced their own radio and television programs, records, plays, films, periodicals, and various types of locally published books (children's books, volumes of poetry, works of scholarship, instructional materials for courses in Cajun French and Cajun culture and history)—all of which focus on the Cajun experience. For instance, Cote Blanche Productions of Cut Off (Bayou Lafourche) has released films about local historical events that use local people as actors. Among these films are *La Fièvre Jaune (Yellow Fever)* and *Huit Piastres et Demie! ($8.50 a Barrel!)*, both in Cajun French with English subtitles.

During the 1970s and early 1980s ethnic consciousness in south Louisiana also manifested itself in an informal tee-shirt-and-bumper-sticker campaign focusing on the word *Coonass*. *Coonass* was originally an ethnic slur used by outsiders to refer to Cajuns. The word is of disputed origin, and it apparently did not appear in Louisiana until after World War II. *Coonass* was an insulting term that implied all the stereotypical, negative qualities associated with Cajuns by some outsiders and some insiders since the nineteenth century: alleged ignorance, laziness, poverty, inefficiency, and excessive indulgence in play and pleasure. However, in a gradual process that began at least as early as the 1960s, some Cajuns inverted the use and the negative connotations of the term, proclaiming themselves to be "Proud Coonasses" and emphasizing an exaggerated earthy, playful and sometimes rowdy image of Cajun life. The phrases "Proud Coonass" and "Registered Coonass, State of Louisiana" adorned countless tee-shirts, hats, decals, bumper stickers, and souvenir trinkets throughout south Louisiana, usually with an accompanying illustration of a rear view of a raccoon with its tail upraised. The display of such items not only indicated pride in being a Coonass, or in being a Cajun, but it also indicated a bit of irreverence toward outsiders and toward the Cajun and white Creole elite (see Dorman [1983]; Rickels [1983]).

Ethnic revivalism often brings with it a struggle between different segments of a group over the selection or suppression of symbols used to express ethnic identity (Barth 1969). For example, many Cajuns have never liked the use of *Coonass* as a symbol of Cajun pride. These Cajuns have never identified with the lifestyle associated with the term and consider the word itself to be vulgar and demeaning, whether used by outsiders or Cajuns. Some, but not all, of those who have voiced disapproval of Coonass paraphernalia have belonged to the Cajun elite—sometimes called Genteel Acadians—or to the closely associated French Renaissance organizations (Rickels 1983). The issue of Coonass paraphernalia was a topic of public debate and media attention in Louisiana in the early 1980s. Today, Coonass souvenirs and bumper stickers are hard to find in south Louisiana, and debates among Cajuns as to the acceptability of the Coonass approach to ethnic pride have subsided.

Acadiana today is a modern region, but one that remains distinct from other modern regions of the United States. The interaction between the traditional and the modern and between Cajuns and non-Cajuns has produced a contemporary regional culture that is varied, complex, and full of often startling juxtapositions of the old and the new, the locally unique and the nationally standard.

The landscape itself reflects a modern Cajun lifestyle that is different from those of both traditional south Louisiana and other modern regions of the United States, and that contains elements of both. Much of Acadiana is best described as a heavily industrialized rural area. Oil wells pump in swamps, cane fields, pastures, and subdivisions, while vast petrochemical plants tower over neighboring plantations and small Cajun homesteads. At the time of my field research, before the mid-1980s slump in the oil industry, the economy was booming and the region's cities were rapidly expanding their borders with commercial strips, shopping malls, and housing developments. The bayous that once served as transportation routes for locals had become obstacles to automobile transportation, causing bottlenecks at bridges and daily traffic jams in even the smaller towns.

Local housing in Acadiana today ranges from traditional cottages to the more common modern tract houses, mobile homes, and condominiums. Traditional Acadian/Creole cottages, built of cypress with *bousillage* (mud and moss filling) in the walls, are now sought after for restoration projects. New Cajun houses are sometimes built in a style that combines the modern features of tract housing with the steep roofs and galleries of the Creole/Acadian cottages—but on a much larger scale, with false shutters and false outside stairways leading to nonexistent *garçonnières* (young men's rooms). A statue of the Virgin Mary is a very common yard accessory for both the newer and older homes.

English is the predominant language in Acadiana today, though French is still commonly spoken also among middle-aged and older people. Despite the efforts of the French Renaissance movement, French as a first language learned in the home seems to be fast disappearing. Yet language continues to distinguish Cajuns from others today: the characteristic Cajun English dialect or accent is omnipresent.

Almost all Cajuns today are Catholic. The Catholic church plays an important role in the lives of individuals in modern Acadiana. Major events in people's lives are marked by church ritual, and even those Cajuns who do not regularly attend services seldom renounce their faith or affiliate with another church. Local churches are a focus of community organization, and Cajuns strongly support church-related clubs, schools, fairs, and fund-raising activities.

Keeping up close kinship ties is important to contemporary Cajuns. The modernization that has sometimes separated family members has also provided the improved communications and transportation network that allows them to keep in touch. For example, Acadiana's colleges are known as "suitcase colleges," because each weekend many of their students drive to their hometowns to be with their families and old friends. Family-run businesses are still common. Some Cajun college students major in fields they say will help them to improve their family businesses in the future, such as agriculture, agronomy, business administration, and accounting. Family residential compounds or neighborhoods are not uncommon today. Some are the products of years of property division among succeeding generations, while others are recent creations. It is not uncommon in Acadiana to see, standing in the yard of a modern house, one or more mobile homes—the residences of newlywed children or elderly parents of the property owner. Cajuns are appalled by the idea of "old folks' homes," and Cajun children today are often close to their grandparents, both geographically and emotionally (Allain 1978). Deceased relatives are not forgotten. Family members visit and maintain gravesites year-round, and All Saints' Day is still a special time for whitewashing tombs, a group task that brings the living together, in remembrance of their dead.

Cajun men and women today participate in all the common modern American occupations, as well as modernized versions of traditional Cajun occupations, such as agribusiness/farming or commercialized/ mechanized fishing. Some practice traditional occupations in a modern marketplace. For example, hunters serve as guides for sportsmen, craftspeople sell their wares to tourists, traditional cooks work at restaurants or as caterers, and musicians make recordings for national distribution. It is common for people to acquire certain products directly from the environment through gardening, fishing, and hunting, but few are primarily involved in a subsistence economy.

Oil is the mainstay of south Louisiana's economy, and it is difficult to overestimate the enormous impact of the petrochemical industry on modern Cajun life. The petrochemical industry is the region's largest employer, and as such it influences the well-being of most (if not all) other business enterprises in the area. At the time of my field research in the late 1970s and early 1980s, the Louisiana oil industry was healthy, the south Louisiana economy was booming, and Cajuns were enjoying increased incomes, low unemployment rates, and business growth (Bradshaw 1977). Layoffs of petrochemical workers began in Louisiana in 1981, and by the mid-1980s the state's economy was seriously depressed.

For much of this century, Cajuns and others in south Louisiana tended to view the petrochemical industry as a savior: it had rescued them from the crop failures of the 1920s and the economic depression of the 1930s, and continued to offer them unprecedented opportunities. However, worsening environmental and health problems, including an extremely high cancer rate in south Louisiana, have prompted local people to reevaluate governmental and corporate policies in the region and to demand improvements. Regional media coverage of environmental and health problems greatly increased during the 1980s, as did the number of environmental defense groups in the area. Injunctions, lawsuits, and even occasional demonstrations have been aimed at corporations and the government. Younger Cajuns, raised in a more environmentally conscious

America, are particularly concerned about pollution and its effects on their land and their lives.

Tourism has become increasingly important in Acadiana. The completion of Interstate 10 in 1973 opened up the region for visitors. The 1984 World's Fair in New Orleans brought additional attention to Cajun culture, as did the flurry of travel writers who visited Acadiana in the mid-1980s. Many of today's visitors are seeking "cultural tourism," in the form of an encounter with Cajuns and their culture. (Ancelet n.d.). Attempts to make this culture accessible to tourists have resulted in a variety of attractions, including restaurants that have live Cajun bands seven days a week; folk heritage projects, such as Vermilionville in Lafayette, which feature traditional skills and arts; cooking schools, where in two hours visitors can learn to make gumbo—and eat it; swamp and bayou boat tours, which advertise close-up views of alligators and cypress trees, seafood-processing plants, netmakers, and "real Cajuns" who speak French for the visitors; and Jean Lafitte National Historic Park, dedicated to preserving both cultural and natural resources. Lafitte Park includes the restored Liberty Theater in Eunice, where a weekly live French-language radio show plays to crowds that are 80 percent local.

Cajuns today are well aware that outsiders have tended to stereotype them in two ways, either as wholesome, peaceful peasants living in an idyllic rural setting, or as ignorant, mysterious, and sometimes violent people inhabiting forbidding swampland (Conrad 1983). Both views portray Cajuns as untouched by the modern world. These stereotypes have not disappeared among non-Cajuns, and they still occasionally appear in the national media.

Cajuns are often amused by tourists who express surprise or dismay when they find that Cajuns ride in cars far more often than in boats, or that Cajuns buy their clothes at department stores rather than making them from traditional textiles, or that Cajuns spend more time playing video games than telling old French folktales. During my field work, a California-based cable television crew arrived in Breaux Bridge, looking for what they called "quaint" Cajun subjects who would "wear bonnets" in their documentary program. One local person said that some outsiders would be less disappointed if Cajuns "lived in a heritage museum."

Cajuns may smile at the ignorance of outsiders who think of modern Acadiana in terms of Longfellow's *Evangeline*, but they are disturbed or angered by less benign forms of stereotyping. For example, *Southern Comfort*, a 1981 Hollywood film, portrayed Cajuns as murderous, territorial swamp dwellers and as hedonistic peasants living in what one Cajun assessed as "Dogpatch in the Atchafalaya Basin." *Southern Comfort* was aptly billed by its producers as the "Cajun *Deliverance*"—a reference to an earlier film that similarly stereotyped people of the southern Appalachians. A 1980 television film, *Dangerous Voyage*, depicted Cajuns as beret-wearing bandits with continental French accents, modern-day pirates who ply the Gulf of Mexico in shrimp boats in order to rob, rape, and murder the crews of pleasure craft. The main character in the film tells one of his victims that Cajuns are the descendants of Acadians, who migrated to Louisiana, joined Jean Lafitte's band of pirates, and continued to practice piracy as an occupation. He also explains that his obviously mentally impaired nephew is a product of "the incestuous inbreeding of our people." Many Cajuns have expressed the belief that any film that portrayed better-known ethnic groups in such a negative manner would be banned from television.

More recently, a 1986 article in *Southern Magazine* scornfully portrayed Cajuns as Atchafalaya swamp dwellers, devoid of "Anglo-Saxon discipline." Making clear his disapproval of positive coverage of contemporary Cajuns in the national media, the author writes:

> With the Cajuns . . . the media's fan letters failed to mention the years of animosity and hostility and suspicion of the outside world that had boiled up in these people. Their lives had given license to the anarchy of the swamp, the brutal rule of law by which it was every man for himself. The adulation overlooked the fact that, like all historically oppressed and ostracized people, the Cajuns shared a universal dream of retribution for their years of suffering and denial, a desire for a day of atonement when one of their own would crawl forth from the swamp and rise to a position of power and redemption. (Greene 1986:76)

Cajuns today pay special attention to such misconceptions about Cajuns in the national media. As modern Americans, Cajuns read the magazine articles, see the movies, and watch the television shows about Cajuns made by outsiders, and they are sometimes displeased. They know that stereotypes perpetuated by the media reach millions of people, and they know that Cajuns do not receive "equal time" in the national forum to refute or clarify assertions made about them. Locals claim that hostile or condescending outsiders are less common in Acadiana than they were twenty years ago (although they do exist), and many outsiders in Acadiana are fascinated by Cajuns and their culture. However, the national media sometimes serve as ephemeral "outsiders" who can insult or misrepresent Cajuns with impunity. Cajuns cannot usually defend their reputation or assert their own identity through the national media, but they can encourage the amorphous "national audience" to come to Acadiana for a first-hand encounter with Cajuns and their lifestyle. Tourism is important to Acadiana symbolically as well as economically: it offers an opportunity for Cajuns to educate the general public (including their own children) about Cajun culture, and it allows Cajuns to express their group identity in their own way to a national and international audience.

CONTEMPORARY CAJUN IDENTITY

There is no short and simple definition of *Cajun* that readily identifies all people who call themselves Cajun. Contemporary Cajun identity is varied, evolving, and complex.

Contact with other groups provides a basis of contrast and self-differentiation, helping people to define their own group identity. For this reason, ethnic identity among Cajuns is stronger today than it was before the increased Americanization and modernization of the twentieth century. The contemporary Cajuns who have the most difficulty in answering the question, What is a Cajun? are those elderly people who have led traditional lives, remaining relatively untouched by Americanization. They frequently respond with puzzlement: "Cajuns? We're all Cajuns around here." One elderly woman's response is typical of those given by other elderly Cajuns: "You didn't hear so much about Cajuns when we were young. We were just old-fashioned, country people. It wasn't a big deal like it is now." Such responses indicate that Cajuns have become more self-consciously *Cajun* as their contact with outsiders has increased; the chronology of Cajun ethnic revivalism suggests that this self-consciousness strengthened (and became a positive identity for a much greater number of Cajuns) after World War II. (For a detailed historical study of the development of Cajun ethnic identity in Louisiana, see James H. Dorman's *The People Called Cajuns: An Introduction to an Ethnohistory*, published in 1983.)

Although Cajuns sometimes disagree about which traits identify them best, certain refrains are frequently heard when Cajuns discuss what it means to be Cajun and when they use symbols to express ethnicity. Cajuns identify themselves by their ancestry, their language, their region, their competence in the natural environment, and their sociability.

ACADIAN ANCESTRY

Cajuns claim descent from the eighteenth-century Acadian refugees. Many if not most Cajuns have Acadian surnames or know of ancestors who had Acadian surnames. Common Cajun surnames serve as ethnic markers—that is, they are generally recognized as Cajun names. For example, Boudreaux, Broussard, Guidry, Hebert, Mouton, and Thibodaux—to name a few—are generally considered by both Cajuns and non-Cajuns to be typically Cajun names. In Acadiana today, a white person who bears one of these names is indeed likely to categorize himself or herself as Cajun. The same is true regarding a number of French names of non-Acadian origin, as well as common Gallicized names of Spanish and German origin, such as Domingue (originally the Spanish Dominguez) and Folse (originally the German Foltz). Some Cajuns bear surnames of Anglo-American and Irish origin, such as Tate, Reed, O'Brien, McGee, and Collins. Partial descent from other European (and sometimes Native American) groups does not stop people from identifying themselves, and being recognized by others, as Cajuns. Similarly, possessing a non-Acadian surname does not exclude a person from being Cajun.

However, a person who has African ancestry is not classified as a Cajun by Cajuns, even though that person may also have Acadian ancestry, may have an Acadian name, may have lived in Acadiana all his life, may share many cultural traits (including the French language) with Cajuns, and, in some cases, may be indistinguishable in appearance from Cajuns. Afro-French students at the University of Southwestern Louisiana have complained about the name of the school's athletic teams—Ragin' Cajuns— since the early 1970s. They too say that *Cajun* refers only to whites, and they have displayed bumper stickers proclaiming, "Cajun—It Just Ain't Us" and "Ragin' Un-Cajuns" (see Dorman 1983:78).

Ethnic jokes about Cajuns, told by both Cajuns and non-Cajuns, often feature a stereotyped Cajun character who has a "typical" Cajun surname as well as a "typical" Cajun given name. Typical Cajun given names include French names and also Gallicized Greek and Roman names, such as Aristide and Telesphore—the legacy of classically educated French priests. Also typical are nicknames acquired during childhood, which are often used exclusively during adulthood. Some adults in Breaux Bridge do not know the "real" names even of their close friends; for this reason, the local telephone directory includes nicknames in its listings, enclosed in parentheses and following the given name. Examples of such nicknames are Papit, Neg, 1/2 pint, Te Noo, Nu, Coon, Gabby, Goon, Nookie, Boo Boo, and Pep.

Acadian families in Louisiana often passed down knowledge of their Acadian origins to later generations, thereby keeping alive a self-perceived distinction between their origins and those of other French groups in Louisiana. However, it is likely that any Acadian families who may have lost knowledge of their origins regained it after the publication in 1847 of Longfellow's *Evangeline: A Tale of Acadia* and the subsequent regional acceptance of the poem's fictional heroine as the "symbol of the Acadian diaspora" (Rushton 1979:263).

Today virtually every Cajun knows some version of the story of Evangeline and, consequently, the fictionalized story of the Acadian exile— from Longfellow's poem, or from the 1929 Hollywood film, or from oral tradition. Streets, businesses, and local product brands are named for Evangeline, and her picture appears on labels, on billboards, in the Yellow Pages of local telephone directories, and in tourism brochures. In St. Martinville, a locality mentioned in the poem, one citizen maintained for years a combination general store, souvenir stand, and shrine to Evangeline, which he founded shortly after World War I (Kane 1943:262–64). St. Martinville is the site of a monument popularly referred to as the "tomb" of the "real" Evangeline, an Acadian exile named Emmeline Labiche, whose story is claimed by some locals to have been the source of Longfellow's inspiration. St. Martinville is also the site of the Evangeline Oak, under which, according to local legend, Evangeline/Emmeline met her long-lost fiancé. There are Acadian heritage museums and villages in St. Martinville, Lafayette, Loreauville, and elsewhere.

Some older Cajuns today know the historical texts as well as the literary and popular sources of information concerning their origins, and younger

Cajuns have studied their history in school. Cajun teenagers discuss the Acadian exile in a manner that indicates a personal, emotional involvement in their group's history, not unlike the way southerners recount the events of the Civil War and Reconstruction. In recent decades Cajuns in Louisiana have met their Canadian Acadian "cousins" in large numbers for the first time in over two centuries. CODOFIL has hosted groups of Canadian Acadians visiting Louisiana, sometimes arranging for them to stay in Cajun homes. Some Cajuns who can afford international travel have elected to visit Canada and France, to see their ancestral homelands. Young Cajun intellectuals, inspired by these travels and by the results of Alex Haley's visits to Africa (recounted in his *Roots*), say that *Evangeline* is the Cajun *Uncle Tom's Cabin*, and that there is a now a need for a Cajun parallel to *Roots*, a book and/or film that would follow a Cajun family from its origins in Acadia to contemporary Acadiana.

LANGUAGE

When the Acadian settlers arrived in Louisiana, the Acadian French they spoke undoubtedly marked them as different from other French speakers in the colony. Later shifts in dialect and language among their descendants and among non-Acadians in Louisiana have made the speaking of Acadian French a rather poor indicator of Cajun identity today.

For those Cajuns who speak French today, the particular dialect they speak is not what determines whether they are of Cajun or non-Cajun French ethnicity, although dialect is associated with class distinctions. For example, a Cajun who speaks French Creole is not "disqualified" from claiming Cajun identity, although he may insist that he speaks "bad" French, and many Cajuns are likely to agree. Regardless of their particular dialect, many Cajuns say that their French is not "good" or "real" (that is, standard) French. They identify standard French speakers as a group separate from themselves: they call white Creoles and tourists from France "*real* French people." A local priest has observed that a Cajun who speaks standard French to other Cajuns, or who talks about his non-Cajun French ancestors, is thought by others to be "putting on the dog."

Both Cajun and non-Cajun French speakers in south Louisiana have traditionally distinguished themselves as *Frenchmen* or *French people,* terms that refer to *all* native French speakers, including Cajuns, white French Creoles, black French Creoles, and Creoles of color. The term

French people (not to be confused with *real French people*, a distinction that is usually evident from context) contrasts with the term *Americans (les Americains)*, a term that refers to language (English), to personal or ancestral point of origin (anywhere in the United States except south Louisiana), and to religion (Protestantism) (see Tentchoff 1975:88–92). Younger Cajuns use the term *American* (in contrast to *Frenchman*) less frequently than do older Cajuns. Those who do use the traditional terminology point out that their use of *American* to refer to a group separate from themselves does not mean that they do not consider themselves to be U.S. citizens, or that they are not patriotic.

In the past, the speaking of some form of French was the most prominent characteristic that distinguished Cajun and other French-speaking south Louisianans from non-French-speaking outsiders. For those Cajuns who speak French today, the language is still an important identity marker that distinguishes them from outsiders as well as from more "modern" and often younger or more urbanized Cajuns. The French language is the language of intimate settings—the home and the community—and of the old days.

The French language has also served in other capacities during times of rapid sociocultural change. Numerous young adults recall that their parents did not allow their children to speak French. These parents spoke French as a secret language in front of their children, when they did not want the children to understand the adult conversation. Similarly, French-speaking schoolchildren used the language to exclude English-speaking teachers from their conversations, and French-speaking employees used it to exclude English-speaking employers.

Some French-speaking Cajuns are proud of their language, some are neutral toward it, and some are ashamed of it. For proponents of the French Renaissance movement, the speaking of French is the most important symbol of Cajun ethnic identity and of a more general regional French identity. However, some Cajuns consider French an inappropriate symbol because of its sometimes still-lingering associations with ignorance or poverty of the past. For many others—those monolingual English-speaking Cajuns—the speaking of French as an expression of ethnic identity simply is not possible, at least not without a great deal of studious effort.

A Cajun who speaks no French is not considered to be any less a Cajun than is a French-speaking Cajun. In fact, the speaking of Cajun English is an important identity marker for both bilingual Cajuns and monolingual English-speaking Cajuns. Most English-speaking Cajuns have a readily recognizable Cajun English "accent" or dialect that is distinguished by pronunciation ("accent") and sometimes by the occasional use of French words and French-derived grammatical constructions and intonations. Cajun ethnic jokes, when told in English rather than in French, are told in the Cajun English dialect, and sometimes the dialect itself is the subject of the joke. Both Cajuns and non-Cajuns tell these jokes, which suggests that both insiders and outsiders view Cajun English as a "typically Cajun" trait.

Some Cajuns are ashamed of their nonstandard English, but most are not. Some, especially the middle-aged and older generations, say that their nonstandard English has hurt them in employment and educational settings. Some individuals intensify their accents in situations where being a Cajun is an asset—for example, when talking with outsiders who are known to be interested in Cajun culture, or when taking part in public events that celebrate Cajun ethnicity. Male college students have told me that they consciously exaggerate their accents when vacationing at resorts outside of Acadiana, in order to attract the attention of non-Cajun women, who are allegedly fascinated by the Cajuns' unconventional style of speech.

REGIONAL ORIGIN

In response to the question, What is a Cajun? Cajuns frequently define themselves as "people from around here" or "people from south Louisiana [or Acadiana]." Further questioning reveals that not all people from the region are Cajuns, but rather all Cajuns are from the region.

Most Cajuns today do live in south Louisiana, and those who do not often maintain social and cultural ties with the region. For example, Cajuns who moved for employment to coastal Mississippi or southeastern Texas in the first half of this century today attend family reunions in south Louisiana. Stores in both localities stock Cajun foodstuffs and Cajun recordings. Cajuns who live in coastal Mississippi maintain an ethnic/fraternal organization, and Cajuns in Port Arthur, Texas, host a Cajun heritage festival similar to those that take place in Acadiana. Contiguous with Acadiana, the Beaumont–Orange–Port Arthur triangle of southeastern Texas has been referred to by Cajuns as "Cajun Lapland"—the area where Louisiana "laps over" into Texas (Rickels 1983).

Regional and ethnic labels used by Cajuns and non-Cajuns indicate that Cajun identity blends with regional identity. The geographic area where Cajuns live is referred to as Acadiana, Cajun country, and French Louisiana, and Cajuns are sometimes referred to as south Louisianans or bayou people. Cajuns have a strong sense of place and often describe themselves as uncomfortable or unhappy when away from the region for a long time. Although today's Cajuns are not as home-oriented as their ancestors described by nineteenth-century observers, there are many older Cajuns and some younger Cajuns who have never left south Louisiana. Most Cajun college students attend college in Acadiana, and a sizeable minority select schools in Baton Rouge or New Orleans. Few choose to attend colleges outside of south Louisiana. Local newspapers sometimes publish letters to the editor from expatriated Cajuns, telling of their homesickness. A Cajun artist explained his emotional attachment to his region in these words:

> In my case, I had to leave Louisiana three times looking for happiness. I happened to have found it in the marshes of Belle Isle, below Intracoastal. I've gone to Los Angeles, Houston, San Francisco, Ilwaco and several other places, but all I found was loneliness.
>
> You know what brought me back? I wanted to hear about boudin and crawfish and sauce piquante, and more than anything else, I wanted to taste them. That's it, that's our people, our culture, our love of nature, our needs. That's what happiness is all about . . . fishing on our bayous, watching the full moon on Belle Isle Ridge, spending the night on Chenier-au-Tigre, going to Pecan Island to Broussard's Bar and talking to the locals. That's what life is all about. It's not just existence anymore when you do that. Existence is Houston, New York, and San Francisco. Life is Louisiana. (Broussard 1982:6)

Do Cajuns identify themselves as southerners? Some Breaux Bridge natives say that Cajuns never refer to themselves as southerners, and others say that Cajuns are both Cajuns and southerners. Cajuns rarely spontaneously refer to themselves as southerners, but Cajuns do use the word *Yankee* to refer to nonsoutherners. However, Cajuns also occasionally use *Yankee* to refer to southerners, sometimes jokingly, sometimes apparently seriously. A Breaux Bridge resident explains the latter usage:

"We call people Yankees if they're not from here, whether they're from New York or north Louisiana. To us, both come from the North." The term *redneck*, though, is more commonly applied to southerners than is *Yankee*. During the early days of the oil industry, all southerners were called *Texans (Texiens)* in some parts of south Louisiana (Kammer 1941:87; Kane 1944:258). Thus Cajuns have used terms that mark southerners as people from another, separate region (*redneck*, *Texan*, and sometimes *Yankee*), but they also use *Yankee* to refer to people who are neither Cajuns nor southerners, a usage that implies that both Cajuns and southerners belong to the seldom-named category of southerners (that is, non-Yankees).

The ambiguity of southern identity among Cajuns is also revealed by their *partial* sharing of the myths or symbols that unify southerners as a group (see Hill [1977]). Like other white southerners, Cajuns say that the Civil War was "lost" rather than "won," a choice of words that indicates the direction of their sympathies. Older people in Breaux Bridge say that "Civil War consciousness" was once higher than it is today, and they tell anecdotes about battles along Bayou Teche, "Yankee pillaging" in Breaux Bridge, and vigilante activity during Reconstruction. In their recounting of these aspects of their history, the "Yankees" are clearly cast as villains. Like many white southerners, many Cajuns say that integration was forced on their communities by outsiders who "hypocritically" ignored racism in their own communities, and they point out that national media coverage of "race relations" in Louisiana and other southern states has focused primarily on events that support the stereotype of white southerners as racists.

Although Cajuns affiliate with the white southern view of American history, the use of public symbols derived from this view of history is rare in Acadiana, compared to such use in the American South. For example, the statues of Confederate soldiers and other war memorials so common in small southern towns are rare in Acadiana. To my knowledge, Confederate Memorial Day is not celebrated in Acadiana. The display of the Confederate battle flag is not nearly as ubiquitous as the display of the flag of Acadiana. "Jolie Blonde" (a traditional Cajun song sometimes referred to as the "Cajun national anthem"), "Jambalaya (On the Bayou)" (also sometimes referred to as the Cajun national anthem), and "The Battle of New Orleans" (a song about the British invasion of Louisiana in 1814) receive rousing responses at Cajun festivals—while "Dixie" is rarely played at all. Pictures of Evangeline dressed in peasant garb (or of young women dressed in Evangeline costumes) are more common in tourist-oriented publications and settings than are similar representations of the antebellum "southern belle" image. As far as public symbolism is concerned, Cajun identity receives more attention than does southern identity. I know of no widely accepted symbol that encompasses both Cajun and southern identity, although the interpretation of local history given by one highly educated Breaux Bridge native merges a Cajun view of history with a southern view: "The law against speaking French was passed by the descendants of the carpetbaggers and scalawags. They wanted to punish Louisianians, even after Reconstruction was over, by forcing them to adopt Anglo ways."

The relative weakness of southern identity among Cajuns is probably due to the fact that the Cajun experience only partially overlaps with the southern experience. Cajuns share with southerners an attachment to the land, an emphasis on kinship, the social legacies of slavery, a sense of having been defeated in a war and in the national political arena, and a perception of themselves as a minority group that has never fully participated in or been fully understood by the American mainstream (see Hill [1977:309–14]; and Woodward [1960:24–31]). On the other hand, the southern Protestant world view and its characteristic symbols, rituals, and rules for individual behavior are foreign to Cajuns (see Peacock [1975:197–203]).

Of course, the Cajun collective experience has contained elements, in addition to Catholicism, that are foreign to the southern collective experience: a history of exile; a French linguistic and cultural heritage; adaptation to an atypically southern natural environment; adjustment to a multi-ethnic, heterogeneous social environment; and a relatively early and widespread industrialization. These elements provide a basis for contrast between Cajuns and other southerners, and their existence precludes a strong southern identity among Cajuns.

ENVIRONMENTAL COMPETENCE

Cajuns frequently describe themselves in terms of their competence within the south Louisiana natural environment. The extremely fertile natural environment of Acadiana allows a great variety of plant and animal life to flourish; the region also has rich mineral resources. Cajuns have learned many skills, some of them unique to the area, to exploit the abundant and varied resources of their region. The local environment, especially the swamps and marshes, is often challenging and sometimes hazardous. Cajuns know the problems and dangers of life in their environment and know how to minimize them. Cajuns—especially, but not exclusively, male Cajuns—describe themselves as people who know where the good fishing spots are, who know how to track game, who are skilled marksmen, who can handle horses and boats, and who are able to travel through the swamps and marshes without getting lost. Outsiders, by contrast, are stereotyped as people who are less competent than Cajuns in dealing with the local environment.

In the late 1930s, a sociologist observed that status among Cajun men on Bayou Lafourche was largely determined by physical skills, many of which were related to environmental competence. "Prestige is earned by purely physical accomplishments. The man who can shoot better than his neighbors, paddle a pirogue faster, run a bigger trap line, tong more oysters, or hold more liquor, is admired for these accomplishments . . . a priest receives what almost amounts to homage because he is a crack shot. . . . It follows, of course, that physical courage is ranked first among the virtues (Kammer 1941:33)." Kammer adds that the locals distinguished courage from foolhardiness: men who would crush the heads of poisonous water moccasins with their heels did not dare venture out in their fishing boats in bad weather.

Of course, many Cajuns nowadays do not make a living through the land- and water-based occupations that demand competence in the local environment. Today, however, such environmental skills have become important in recreational as well as occupational settings. Most Cajuns, even the city dwellers, have access to rural areas, and those who do not actually live in rural areas make an effort to spend their leisure time there. For example, many urban and small-town Cajuns own "camps"—second homes in rural areas where family and friends gather on weekends or holidays to fish, hunt, and socialize. Some rural Cajuns also own camps in addition to their first homes in the country. The ownership of camps is an old practice, which has its roots in the traditional occupations that required people to spend long periods of time in isolated areas. Camps are strongly associated with male socializing. Ownership of a camp is not an indicator of wealth; camps may be simple and unpretentious or "fancy" and expensively (but casually) furnished. Many Cajun families own boats, pickup trucks, and/or four-wheel-drive vehicles, all of which are useful for gaining access to isolated areas and for carrying equipment and the day's catch. Cajun men eagerly anticipate the opening of hunting season each year. The event produces a flurry of activity at sporting goods stores and receives thorough coverage in the local media.

Cajuns' image of themselves as competent in the local environment is sometimes expressed symbolically in public settings. For example, festivals that celebrate Cajun ethnicity often include contests or demonstrations of locally useful skills, such as skinning furs, opening oysters, calling ducks, carving duck decoys, racing pirogues, and riding horses. A tee shirt sold in Acadiana in the early 1980s portrayed a "Louisiana Coonass" as a man with webbed feet wearing an array of fishing and hunting equipment. Customized vans with names such as Cajun Country and Louisiana Rider are decorated with hunting or fishing motifs and swamp or marsh scenes.

Cajuns themselves and oil industry managers claim that the Cajuns' ability to function successfully in the sometimes hazardous natural environment of Louisiana contributes to their success as "hands on" workers in the oil industry, especially in the swamps and marshes and offshore (Bradshaw 1977:31). In south Louisiana, industrial facilities are often located in these challenging natural settings. Cajuns identify themselves as especially good at working in such settings. On Bayou Lafourche, Cajuns first became involved in the oil industry by applying their traditional skills and knowledge in service to the industry: they used their fishing trawlers to transport freight to and from oil fields along Bayou Lafourche (Kammer 1941:161). Lang quotes a local man's explanation of why Cajuns became successful oil field workers:

> We were blessed by the fact that this new industry needed skills that we knew best and took traits that were bred into Cajuns to survive. . . . Cajuns were not afraid of risk because they lived with that daily; death by drowning was an expected end of life. They were used to failure—hurricanes periodically wiped away all they had. What they lacked in training they compensated for in instinct. I've seen steel crew boats, as seaworthy as the best, designed on the back of a napkin. (quoted in Lang 1978:32)

Today, oil field work, either offshore or "on the bank" (on shore) is identified as a typical Cajun occupation by both Cajuns and outsiders.

The image of the modern Cajun industrial-rural working environment and of the skills required to function in it is clearly illustrated in a full-page advertisement for Cameron Iron Works in *Acadiana Profile,* a regional magazine that focuses on both the Cajun heritage and the local petrochemical industry. The advertisement consists of a large color photograph of a man in an industrial jumpsuit, paddling a boat through a dark grove of moss-draped cypress trees. The photograph is accompanied by the following copy:

> The swamp gripped me like it meant to never let go. Even the water moccasins could get lost in the morning bayou fog. And the smoke from my outboard had been thicker than the mist when I had to shut it off. So I breathed a heavy sigh of relief when I spotted the Bestin Piroux.
>
> She was a DL-12 rig barge backed up in a dredger cut. From the boat I could see swamp spiders infested everything. Webs hung so thick the crew had to cut tunnels through them to operate the equipment.
>
> "Nice place," I said to the company man. "You haven't seen anything," he smiled back. Heavy rains had brought alligators. Six and eight footers, some of which found their way into the barge's central slot where we had to work.
>
> I began thinking the spiders mean to gift wrap me for the 'gators when the cook started throwing chicken bones off the stern. I figured they must taste better than a Cameron service hand, because the 'gators cleared the keyway with a fury.
>
> The completion was smooth and the crew sharp. I was glad to learn the crew boat would take me back down the channel before dark. "Thanks for keeping those 'gators occupied while I worked," I told the old Cajun cook. "I'm gonna told you man," he said. "I be bringing 'em 'round. That young 'gator tail be good eating, don't you know."

The advertisement is signed with the slogan, "Cameron—Men of Iron." The advertisement does not tell the reader exactly what the company's product or service is, or why Cameron Iron Works is better than competing companies. Rather, the company identifies itself with an image that is identified with and understood by the Cajun readers. The ad assumes that readers understand industrial jargon ("DL-12 rig barge," "dredger cut," "keyway") and are familiar with a work environment that includes alligators, water moccasins, swamp spiders, and potentially treacherous fog. The old Cajun cook knows how to control alligators (and knows what parts are good to eat), and the men on the scene are a "sharp" crew.

Cajuns sometimes stereotype outsiders as people who are not competent in the local environment, in contrast to themselves. One very common joke, told by Cajuns in a number of versions, portrays the pompous city slicker as someone who gets hopelessly lost in the local countryside (Reed 1976:99). In another joke, the outsider must rely on a Cajun to pull his car out of the mud; in one version the Cajun says to the outsider, " 'Course you is city fellow and you don't know damn thing anyway' " (Saxon, Dreyer, and Tallant 1945:205). The Cajuns' possession of skills and knowledge learned in the Louisiana environment has led to one particularly satisfying triumph over outsiders. As one man explains it, "The British didn't want us in Canada, so they kicked us out. Now they're begging Cajuns to come to England—and paying a lot—to help them in the North Sea [offshore oil fields]. They couldn't get that oil without us."

Both men and women identify Cajuns as environmentally competent, although this image of Cajuns relates primarily to men. In its extreme form, the expression of this aspect of Cajun identity involves "macho" and sometimes violent imagery, as in the lyrics of musician Doug Kershaw's "Cajun Joe (The Bully of the Bayou)":

People still talk about Cajun Joe.
Cajun Joe, he was the bully of the bayou.
He'd fight anything, a beast or man
In bayou water or on dry land.

Some Cajuns dislike such imagery because it is consistent with the negative stereotype of Cajuns as violent swamp dwellers.

Although the traditional domain of Cajun women, the home, is a relatively safe environment where the skills derived from masculine occupations are less likely to be needed, environmental competence is not totally irrelevant to the lives of Cajun women. Their homes sometimes have been located in hazardous environments. For example, traditional trappers and their families migrated to camps in the marsh during the trapping season. Women took care of domestic chores and skinned the animals brought home by their husbands. Today some Cajun women work with their husbands or fathers on shrimp boats, many enjoy recreational fishing, and some hunt with their husbands (see Allain [1978:140]).

Cajun women are not expected to be notably fragile or squeamish. Even Evangeline is said to have crossed the dangerous Atchafalaya Basin in a canoe, an event that is reenacted in part at one Cajun heritage festival.

CAJUN SOCIABILITY

Since the early nineteenth century, Cajuns in Louisiana have been described by non-Cajun observers as sociable, fun-loving people, fond of play and dancing. Cajuns today describe themselves as sociable, hospitable, and full of joie de vivre. Cajuns claim to have a unique ability to "enjoy life" and to "have a good time." Symbolic forms used to express Cajun identity are often those associated with "having a good time": music, dancing, foodways, and festivals.

In the early 1940s, field workers for the Louisiana Writers' Project of the Works Progress Administration (WPA) collected from oral tradition the saying that "Cajun heaven is gumbo, go-go, and do-do" (food, sex, and sleep; see Saxon, Dreyer, and Tallant [1945:203]). Today that phrase or some variant of it is found on bumper stickers and tee shirts throughout Acadiana. Elderly people from Breaux Bridge recall how, during the flood of 1927, local residents spent their time in relief camps "having parties and dancing." A middle-aged Cajun woman says, "We party here all the time. We work, play, and make love with equal zeal." A middle-aged Cajun man advises that "to understand the Cajun heritage, you must go to a local dance hall, a cockfight, and the Carencro quarterhorse races." A Cajun priest says that "it is recognized here that you let down your hair on Saturday night."

The Cajun emphasis on having a good time should not be interpreted as an indication that Cajuns value unbridled hedonism. While it is true that some Cajuns may play up this component of Cajun identity, often on purpose to tease or shock outsiders, they recognize the limits on having a good time. Both hard work and hard play are valued, and the latter is usually not allowed to interfere with the former. While some Cajuns may believe that "God winks at a lot of little things" (Lang 1978:32), they do not believe that anything goes. For example, Cajuns, even children, enjoy gambling with family and friends, but few Cajuns approve of people who allow an addiction to gambling to affect adversely their personal and financial stability. Alcohol, especially beer, is commonly consumed with meals, and such use seldom leads to drunkenness. Even in barrooms or dance halls, where people are more likely to drink alcohol for its pleasurable psychological effect, obnoxious or uncontrolled drunkenness is disapproved of. For Cajuns, substance abuse is not an accepted way to "have a good time."

The various activities associated with joie de vivre are, in essence, activities that allow people to enjoy other people's company, often within the context of the extended family:

> The social atmosphere at such gatherings—a lack of repressive attitudes, the free-wheeling gregariousness, enjoyment of life for its own sake, excited wagering on games, wildly funny stories, social and sexual attractions of dancing, and the continual festive atmosphere—all these contribute to the enjoyment of family life and its fundamental dominance of the lives of individual members. (Ancelet, Edwards, and Pitre 1991:73)

Thus, occasions of joie de vivre affirm and nurture group solidarity. For example, the Saturday-night dances for which Cajuns are so famous are strongly rooted in family and community socializing, although most dances today are not family-oriented. In the past, house dances were held wherever there were no dance halls. Around the time of the Louisiana Purchase, the French traveler C. C. Robin observed an Acadian dance, which he described as follows:

> Ordinarily their manner is reserved but they are no strangers to gaiety. They love to dance most of all; more than any other people in the colony. At one time during the year, they give balls for travelers and will go ten or fifteen leagues to attend one. Everyone dances, even *Grandmère* and *Grandpère*, no matter what the difficulties they must bear. There may be only a couple of fiddles to play for the crowd, there may be only four candles for light, placed on wooden arms attached to the wall; nothing but long wooden benches to sit on, and only exceptionally a few bottles of *Tafia* [alcoholic beverage made from sugarcane] diluted with water for refreshment. No matter, everyone dances. But always everyone has a helping of *Gumbo*, the Creole dish *par excellence*; then "Good night," "Good evening," "So Long," "See you next week" (if it isn't sooner). One shoves off in his pirogue, his paddle in hand; another gallops off on horseback, others who live nearer walk home singing and laughing. (Robin 1966:115)

Almost one hundred years later, Charles Dudley Warner visited the LeBlanc family near the coastal marshes of southwestern Louisiana and noted that Mr. LeBlanc had built a "ballroom" on the front of his house, where every two weeks he held neighborhood dances (1889:94). Today, middle-aged and older residents can still recall when Saturday-night dances were family events attended by both children and adults. They say that in their youth courting couples were strictly chaperoned, and polite behavior was expected of all those who attended a dance. The term *fais dodo* (go to sleep) is still used to refer to a Cajun dance, and it harkens back to the time when mothers brought their infants and small children to dance halls and put them to sleep in a separate room or on shelves under the bar. Thus dancing and dance halls in Acadiana have traditionally been associated with controlled, family-oriented behavior. Today, of course, dance halls exist that are aptly described as "singles bars"; they are popular mostly among the young, as is the case elsewhere in the United States. However, the Cajun ethnic revival has brought about a renewed interest in traditional forms of socializing among young people, and young and old now mingle at the older Cajun dance halls or at the newer clubs that are designed and managed in imitation of the older ones. During the 1980s a growing number of combination restaurant/dance halls, such as Mulate's in Breaux Bridge, made it possible for children and adults to dance and enjoy Cajun food in a commercial setting that imitates old family-oriented dance halls. Children, parents, and grandparents also dance together to traditional Cajun music at local festivals, as they did at house dances and fais do-dos in the past.

In the 1930s, a study by sociologists in Louisiana suggested that the "esprit de corps" and "joie de vivre" of Cajuns "engendered imitation" among outsiders; they quoted a "recently acculturated Anglo-Saxon" as saying that the Cajun lifestyle was "easy to catch, and once caught, who in the hell wants to change?" (Smith and Parenton 1938:346). Cajuns today similarly portray their lifestyle as infectious or seductive, easily attracting outsiders. Residents of St. Martin parish still use the phrase "easy to catch," and they also say that once a visitor "drinks water from Bayou Teche" (or "tastes Breaux Bridge coffee" or "eats crawfish"), he or she will never want to leave. A Breaux Bridge woman explains that "people who come here learn to relax and have fun. That's something they don't teach you in north Louisiana." Local people believe that other people admire Cajuns for their sociability and joie de vivre, and such beliefs form an integral part of public expressions of Cajun identity—for example, at festivals and in tourism advertisements. However, Cajuns sometimes express anxiety over this aspect of their identity, worrying that outsiders may interpret Cajun joie de vivre as an indication of laziness and/or hedonism—as indeed some outsiders have done, both in the past and in the present.

Cajuns claim that Protestantism is incompatible with their lifestyle, and they perceive Protestants as the people who are most likely to disapprove of the Cajun lifestyle. Protestants, especially Baptists, are stereotyped by Cajuns as dour people who disapprove of drinking, dancing, gambling, and other forms of "fun." Although the minority of Protestants who actually live in south Louisiana seem to have little power to control or limit their Cajun neighbors' behavior, Protestants have sometimes imposed their values on Cajuns through state and federal laws governing liquor sales, gambling, and the sale of hardware on Sundays. "The trouble with Protestants," says one Cajun, "is that they think that everything that's enjoyable is a sin. We have more of a live and let live attitude." A local Cajun professional woman says she is grateful that "Breaux Bridge has never been tainted by the Protestant ethic."

It is mostly in relation to self-perceived sociability and joie de vivre that Cajuns mention Catholicism as a trait that distinguishes them from outsiders, whom they often assume to be Protestant. Neither Cajuns nor the Catholic church claims that Catholicism *causes* Cajuns to be especially fun-loving; rather, it *allows* them to be that way. The church tolerates activities associated with joie de vivre and even forgives a penitent's excesses, but it does not *demand* that its members dance, drink, or gamble. Although some church parishes do seem to encourage such activities by incorporating them into fund-raising events, such fund-raisers are local activities and not a part of church dogma or ritual.

The distinction between the church's teachings and its tolerance of local custom may be illustrated through carnival and Lenten activities. The church teaches that Lent is a time of penance, and many Cajuns respond to this by attending Mass more frequently (daily, in some instances) and by giving up drinking, dancing, smoking, or favorite foods during Lent. However, the church does not teach that Lent must be preceded by Mardi Gras, or carnival, a time devoted to revelry. Some Catholics, including Cajuns, celebrate carnival season, and others do not. Cajuns usually view Catholic dogma, symbols, and rituals as Catholic rather than as Cajun. The only common symbols that express both Catholic and Cajun identity are St. Ann and Our Lady of the Assumption, both patron saints of the Acadians.

Ethnicity is only one aspect of an individual's identity, and it is only one of many factors that influence a person's life. Cajuns, like other people, identify themselves according to nonethnic factors, such as age, sex, kinship, and occupation, and their lives are filled with a full spectrum of activities and concerns that have nothing to do with their ethnicity.

It is not surprising, then, that Cajun ethnic symbols are often pragmatic ones that are "easily expressed and felt, without undue interference in other aspects of life" (Gans 1979: 205). In addition, ethnic symbols ideally are flexible enough to be acceptable to the great variety of individuals within the group. For example, Cajun music, as a symbol of ethnicity, is pragmatic and flexible in its appeal and the setting where it is presented. One may celebrate ethnicity through music, when one so chooses, without compromising one's nonethnic, personal style (or generational style, or occupational style, etc.) The sound of the music itself is flexible: a variety of musicians satisfies various audiences by performing styles of Cajun music influenced by rock, blues, western swing, and other sources.

In the following chapters we will see that Cajun food, too, is a pragmatic and flexible symbol of Cajun ethnicity. Cajun foodways represent an aspect of traditional life still readily accessible to modern Cajuns. Food is accepted as a positive group symbol by a broad range of Cajuns—and by outsiders as well. The form and flavor of the food itself varies. Because it can be cooked, served, and eaten in so many ways, Cajun food suits the style and preferences of a variety of individual Cajuns, both as a food and as a symbol.

Yet Cajun food is successful as an ethnic symbol for reasons in addition to its practicality. We shall see that relationships among people and relationships between people and nature underlie the effectiveness of food as an ethnic symbol. We shall see how these relationships are highlighted by the preparation, serving, and eating of Cajun food.

What Goes into Cajun Food

How do Cajuns describe "Cajun food"? Not all the foods Cajuns eat are labeled "Cajun." For instance, Cajuns eat steak and baked potatoes, pizza, packaged breakfast cereals, hamburgers, ice cream, and bananas, but none of these is ever described as Cajun food. The fact that a group of people eats a certain food does not make it "ethnic."

When asked to identify Cajun food, Cajuns often answer by listing various local dishes, such as gumbo, étouffée, boudin, sauce picquante, and chicken fricassee, to name a few. These are all *cooked* foods, and they are prepared according to a Cajun style or aesthetic. For example, many Cajuns note that Cajun food is highly seasoned or strong in flavor—a reference to the *aesthetics* of cooking. Some people point directly to the importance of aesthetics, or style. For example, one man says that "anything we cook is Cajun—it's the *way* you cook it that matters." Similarly, a young woman says that "any food can be Cajun food if it's cooked by a Cajun; it will come out Cajun, no matter what." Cajun dishes and cooking aesthetics are described in detail in later chapters.

Cajuns sometimes describe Cajun food by referring to certain ingredients, such as crawfish, seafood, game, okra, rice, red pepper, and dark roast coffee. These ingredients are considered Cajun because they are produced locally (or distributed locally, in the case of dark roast coffee) and because Cajuns consume them frequently and in great quantities.[1] However, when asked about the significance of specific ingredients, people often conclude that cooking style is more important than the use of a particular ingredient. For example, one man who had referred to game as a Cajun food had second thoughts after recalling that he had once eaten Brunswick stew in Georgia. That stew was made from game, but it was definitely not Cajun. In addition, some frequently eaten and locally produced ingredients are described as Cajun only if they are cooked in a particular way. For example, pork and chicken are not necessarily Cajun foods, but boudin (a pork and rice sausage), pork backbone stew, and chicken gumbo or jambalaya *are* Cajun foods. This chapter focuses on ingredients commonly used in preparing Cajun food.

Whether they are referring to specific ingredients or to cooking styles, Cajuns say that Cajun foods are "old-fashioned" or "old-timey." One elderly woman says, "Cajun food is just the kind of food we had when we were young. It's not much different today." An elderly man claims that "Cajun food today is the same as it was fifty or sixty years ago. The only difference is that now you can buy what you need in a grocery store." Younger people, who cannot remember the old days, nonetheless associate Cajun food with the past. They refer to their grandparents or other elders as the best Cajun cooks, and say that they are the people to talk to in order to learn about Cajun food. The young people evaluate their own cooking in terms of old standards. For example, one young woman says that she has been trying for years to make gumbo as good as her mother's. Both young and old describe Cajun food as "part of the Cajun heritage."

The publication of chef Paul Prudhomme's *Louisiana Kitchen* and the New Orleans Worlds Fair, both in 1984, brought a great deal of attention to Cajun food and were accompanied by a flowering of Cajun haute cuisine, often prepared by trained chefs and served in restaurants, or dissiminated through cookbooks and videos. New dishes have been added to the menus of both professional and domestic cooks. In addition, health concerns have prompted the publication of Cajun cookbooks featuring low fat, low calorie, and low salt versions of traditional recipes. The

1. The foodways of non-Cajun south Louisianans are similar to those described in this book. Cajuns recognize this similarity, but they nonetheless describe these foods as "Cajun."

descriptions of Cajun foodways in this book pre-date both these developments. Moreover, these descriptions refer to traditional domestic and community cooking rather than to professional restaurant cuisine.

Outsiders are sometimes confused by the coexistence in south Louisiana of the terms *Cajun food* and *Creole food*. Tourist-oriented restaurants in both Acadiana and New Orleans increasingly advertise their foods as *Cajun-Creole*—a marketing term that suggests a monolithic south Louisiana cuisine (and culture). Indeed, from an outsider's point of view, these two unfamiliar cuisines appear similar, even indistinguishable, especially if the outsider knows local food only through restaurant menus. Cajun chef and author Paul Prudhomme writes that "today, in homes, there is still a distinction between Cajun and Creole cooking; in restaurants, little distinction remains. That's why I've begun referring to the two together as one—Lousiana cooking" (Prudhomme 1984:16).

Many Breaux Bridge residents say that Creole food is the food of New Orleans and its environs. Some say that Creole cuisine is also the food of the wealthy, white French Creoles, including those who live in Acadiana. These uses of the term *Creole food* are consistent with those of the media in both New Orleans and Acadiana, and of the authors of nationally distributed books on regional cuisine in the United States (see, for example, Fiebleman [1971]; and Mitcham [1978]).

From the Cajun point of view, the two cuisines are similar when contrasted with "American" cooking, but differences between the two are evident when they are compared to each other. Although Breaux Bridge residents readily assert that the two cuisines are different, many have difficulty in defining the precise nature of the differences. This may be due to their unfamiliarity with the cuisine they call Creole. Those who can describe the differences between the two cuisines generally agree that Creole dishes—at least from the Breaux Bridge native's point of view—contain less cayenne pepper, more tomato sauce, more garlic, and a greater variety of herbs (basil, thyme, sage, etc.) than do Cajun dishes. (For a discussion of the similarities and differences between Cajun and Creole food, written from the point of view of a New Orleans native who is familiar with both cuisines, see Peter S. Fiebleman's *American Cooking: Creole and Acadian* [1971]. For a discussion of Acadian and Cajun food from a historian's perspective, see Brasseaux [1987]. See also Gutierrez's "Louisiana Traditional Foodways" [1985].

GETTING THE INGREDIENTS

In the past Cajun families took most of their food directly from the environment, through farming, fishing, hunting, and gathering. Elderly Cajuns who grew up in the countryside recall that in their youth, coffee, wheat flour, refined sugar, and rice were the only food products that their families had to purchase, and in some parts of Acadiana, rice was raised by families. Today Cajuns, like other Americans, usually purchase food at retail stores, and these stores stock most, but not all, traditional Cajun foodstuffs. The foods that contemporary Cajuns eat are often raised or caught by an anonymous, commercial professional, and they are processed and distributed to retail stores by a chain of anonymous middlemen. Modern methods of refrigeration, transportation, and preservation have eased the seasonal constraints on foodways in Acadiana as elsewhere, although many people still prefer fresh, local ingredients and eat certain foods according to the old seasons (for example, pork is eaten in winter.) In the past, people's competence in the local environment enabled them to put food on the table; today, a paycheck does the same.

Contemporary food procurement and distribution are not always interconnected with the market economy. For example, wild game animals are not sold in grocery stores. Wild game can be acquired only through hunting, or as gifts from friends or relatives who hunt. Killing one's own game for meat is not necessarily a money-saving activity. One local says he suspects that many Cajun men spend more money on hunting equipment, boats, four-wheel-drive vehicles, and camp maintenance than they "save" through taking "free" game. In addition, other foodstuffs that *can* be purchased at stores are often acquired through more direct means. For example, many Cajuns catch their own freshwater fish, crawfish, and seafood—all of which are readily available at stores. Some people who live in the country raise and butcher their own hogs, cattle, and poultry. Most Cajuns who live in the country and many who live in small towns and even cities raise at least some of their own vegetables, fruits, or poultry.

Foodstuffs—particularly those that have been acquired directly from the local environment—are commonly exchanged through informal family and community distribution systems. When people have an abundance of a particular type of food, because of a successful hunt or a prolific garden, they are likely to give portions of it to members of their extended family and to friends, who return the favor when they are in a similar situation. Thus, many Cajuns, even those who live in urban areas, have access to ingredients taken directly from the local environment through the informal food distribution network. Cooked foods are also distributed in this manner. Cajuns commonly eat at each other's homes, and having a relative or close friend present at a family meal is by no means an unusual or formal occasion. People commonly send portions of surplus cooked food to family members or close friends who are not present at a particular meal. Cooked food also may be exchanged for uncooked foods. For example, a grown son regularly supplies his widowed mother with fresh ducks. She cooks the ducks and returns some of them to him and his family in the form of duck gumbo.

MEAT AND FISH

MEAT FROM DOMESTICATED ANIMALS

Pork has long been a mainstay of the diet of American southerners (Hilliard 1972:92–111; Taylor 1982:21–27). Cajuns share with other southerners a fondness for pork as well as a broad repertoire of methods for preserving and preparing it. Cajuns say that they eat "every part of the hog except the squeal." The pork sections in Breaux Bridge grocery stores offer a large variety of cuts of muscle meat, many of which are appropriate for making gravy-containing stews and étouffées ("smothered" dishes cooked in a closed container) as well as fresh pork liver, stomach, heart, tail, and feet with part of the leg attached. Local grocery stores also sell a variety of preserved or semiprepared pork products, such as sausages, salt pork, pickled pork (an almost totally lean salt pork), hogshead cheese, and cracklings. These are prepared by the store or by local processing plants, some of which operate in conjunction with slaughterhouses. The Opelousas area is known for tasso, a strongly smoked ham used as a seasoning meat.

Although beef is not as commonly eaten as pork, it also is a favorite local meat. A study conducted in Breaux Bridge by a rural sociologist (Steelman 1974:18) indicates that roast beef is one of two high-status foods that are served when people wish to impress their guests (crawfish is the other; see chapter 6). Beef eating is most strongly associated with prairie Cajuns, who live in south Louisiana's major cattle-producing area. The most numerous cuts of beef in Breaux Bridge stores are those used in preparing beef-and-gravy dishes. Liver, heart, tongue, brains, kidney, tripe, and sweetbreads are also sold, as well as beef sausages.

Today people in Breaux Bridge usually purchase beef or pork at local grocery stores, meat markets, or slaughterhouses, which sometimes have retail outlets. It is not uncommon for Cajuns who live in the countryside to raise their own hogs and cattle. They may butcher the animals themselves, or they may take them to one of the many small, often family-owned slaughterhouses, which butcher the meat to the owner's specifications and also store it temporarily if necessary.

In the past, meat was butchered and distributed through the cooperative institution known as the community boucherie. Families who took part in a community boucherie agreed to donate an animal, which was butchered—usually at night or in the early morning in order to avoid heat and flies—by participants known for their butchering skills. The meat was then distributed to all participating families. A week or so later, another family contributed an animal, whose meat was similarly distributed. Thus, each family that took part in the boucherie received a steady supply of fresh meat—something otherwise impossible before refrigeration—while at the same time avoiding the glut of meat that would result from individual family butchering. Family boucheries, at which relatives and close friends help or watch the owner butcher an animal in a relatively festive atmosphere and in exchange for a meal and perhaps some meat, are far more common today than are the old, round-robin, exclusively work-oriented community boucheries. (For further discussion of boucheries, see chapter 7 and Ancelet, Edwards, and Pitre [1991:45–46]; Del Sesto [1975:135–38]; Post [1962:135–37]; and Smith and Post [1937:335–37].)

Chicken and turkey are the common domesticated fowl eaten in Acadiana. People in Breaux Bridge usually purchase these meats, and chicken eggs, at grocery stores. Chicken is sold precut (fryers and chicken parts) or whole (roasting birds), as elsewhere in the United States. Similarly, a customer may purchase a whole roasting turkey or individual packages of parts, including necks or tails. In southwestern Louisiana, turkey is not necessarily a Thanksgiving or Christmas food; it is served year-round at large gatherings, such as wedding receptions or club meetings.

GAME

Although domesticated varieties of some animals normally thought of as "wild" or "game" animals occasionally appear in local markets (rabbits and ducks, for example), the animals discussed in this section are usually acquired directly from the local environment. A family usually acquires game from male family members or friends who hunt. Since many Cajun men hunt, fresh game is abundantly available—but only during the legal hunting seasons.

Wildfowl (teal, mallard, geese, doves, quail), deer, squirrel, and rabbit are favorite and relatively abundant sources of game meat. Less commonly, Cajuns hunt and eat raccoon, opossum, muskrat, nutria (a South American fur-bearing rodent, introduced into Louisiana in the late 1930s), and alligator. Alligator hunting has been legal in some parishes since 1980, and alligator farming—now considered to be a significant part of Louisiana's growing aquaculture industry—has been practiced on a limited basis in some parts of south Louisiana since the 1950s (Morgan 1982:82–87). Alligators traditionally were hunted or raised for their hides, with the meat serving as lagniappe (something extra) for those who chose to eat it. Only since 1980 has a major marketing system for alligator meat developed in Louisiana; in the past, hunters threw away the meat they did not use for themselves and their families. To young Cajuns of today, alligator is a newly available meat that may either be hunted as game or purchased at a seafood market, grocery store, or restaurant. To older Cajuns, alligator is an "old-timey" swampers' food—and quite often a food that had been illegally acquired.

Breaux Bridge natives lament that today it is difficult to find freshwater turtles, either in the environment or in markets. Older people recall when several varieties of turtle were readily available: soft-shell turtles, snapping turtles, alligator snapping turtles, "French" turtles, and a turtle, whose name has been forgotten, that contained "seven different kinds of meat." Even though turtle meat is not as readily available in Breaux Bridge as it once was—partly because turtle fishermen concentrate their efforts on catching or raising turtles for pet stores (Comeaux 1972:89)— it can still be found. Older people recall the days when children searched fields for turtle eggs, which their mothers used to bake cakes. In coastal areas of Acadiana, sea turtle meat and eggs are eaten. Occasionally, sea turtle meat is sold in Lafayette stores as a "gourmet" food.

Bullfrog legs are another popular food in south Louisiana. Commercial frogging is a minor industry in St. Martin Parish, and some individuals catch frogs for personal consumption. However, most people buy cleaned frogs at stores. Because commercial frog meat can be satisfactorily frozen, frog meat is no longer the seasonal summer foodstuff it once was.

SEAFOOD AND FRESHWATER FISH

Fresh and frozen seafoods, such as oysters, shrimp, crabs, and saltwater finfish, are sold at grocery stores and seafood markets and from roadside trucks throughout Acadiana. Coastal-area Cajuns are the only ones who can readily take these foods directly from the environment on a regular basis. Nevertheless, seafood is cheaper in south Louisiana than in more inland parts of the country, and it forms an important and well-liked part of the Cajun diet throughout the region. Modern methods of refrigeration and transportation have made fresh seafood available all over Acadiana. Prairie Cajuns point out that this food was not a common part of their diets in the past. Still, seafood is considered a regional food, and not one that is associated only with coastal dwellers.

In inland areas such as Breaux Bridge, freshwater fish may be taken directly from the environment or purchased at seafood markets and grocery stores. Finfish commonly consumed include catfish, sacalait (crappie), garfish, gaspergou (commonly referred to by locals and on seafood market signs as goo-fish or goo), and a variety of others. The blue crab, generally thought of as a seafood, is found considerably inland, in waterways such as the Atchafalaya. Until the mid-twentieth century, river shrimp were abundant in the Mississippi River. (For a survey of fishing techniques used in the Atchafalaya Basin, the major source of freshwater fish in Breaux Bridge, see Comeaux 1972:31–62; for contemporary interviews and photographs of Atchafalaya life by a native of St. Martin Parish, see G. Guirard 1989.) The crawfish, a small, lobsterlike freshwater crustacean of special significance to Cajuns, is discussed in detail in chapters 4–6.

GRAINS

RICE

A Breaux Bridge teacher says rice is served at least once a day in every Breaux Bridge home. Ethnographic observation and interview data indicate that this is generally true—a day on which this staple is not eaten is exceptional. On Sundays and holidays, two forms of rice may be served at the main meal: rice dressing and plain white rice with gravy. Most of the dishes locals label as typically Cajun and/or favorite dishes contain rice. The rice section in Acadiana supermarkets is noteworthy. About one half of one side of an aisle is stocked with rice—short or medium-grain rice predominates in southwestern Louisiana—and sacks weighing twenty to fifty pounds line the floor in front of the shelves.

The French colonists who first settled in southeastern Louisiana were dismayed to discover that wheat, their favorite grain, would not survive in the humid climate. Although the settlers did learn to like corn, they preferred rice. "The French once used bread chiefly to crumble into soup or milk. This eating habit made them try to make a kind of bread from maize or rice. However, neither was found suitable for soaking in soup of any kind. It seems a substitute was soon found for bread in the form of simple boiled rice, for rice too was a starch which could be added to soup, gumbo, or milk" (Lee 1960:98). The Louisiana French first imported rice, probably from the West Indies, around 1718 (Lee 1960:95; Ginn 1940:7); by 1720, rice fields along the Mississippi River were producing abundant crops (Surrey 1916:267). At the time of the Louisiana Purchase, the French traveler C. C. Robin observed the use of rice by French Louisianians. "Its consumption in this country is prodigious," he wrote. "It is seen on all the tables of the Creoles instead of bread. Boiled rice and cornbread replace wheat completely" (Robin 1966:112). He noted that the newly settled Acadians of the period were raising rice on the banks of the Mississippi River (Robin 1966:114).

Rice cultivation on a small scale reached the prairies of southwestern Louisiana by 1760, but it was not until after 1880, when midwestern German immigrants brought mechanized rice-farming techniques to the prairies, that the southwestern prairies became the major rice-producing region in the state. Prior to the late nineteenth century, "river rice" was grown commercially in southeastern Louisiana, particularly along the Mississippi River. In addition, small farmers throughout Acadiana raised rice in backswamps or in small ponds on the prairies. This rice, for home use only, was called Providence rice, because it was up to Providence to assure that the casually planted and cultivated grain was productive (Lee 1960:89). Those Cajuns who acquired their rice in this manner before the widespread availability of commercial rice treated rice as a special food, one that was eaten only on Sundays or holidays. Rice was special because it was in short supply and was dearly bought: harvests of Providence rice were often small, and hand milling rice with a wooden mortar and pestle was a tedious, time-consuming job that could not be done every day (Lee 1960:110). The oldest people in Breaux Bridge remember when rice was a special, holiday food. They say that during the early years of the twentieth century—and for some families as recently as the 1930s—grits, not rice, was the staple accompaniment for many Cajun dishes. Many members of younger generations, however, have never eaten grits with gumbo, and few Cajuns express regret over the demise of that combination.

CORN

Like pork, corn long has been an important food throughout the southern United States, and Cajuns and other south Louisianans have long raised and eaten corn. Fresh corn, from grocery stores or from gardens, is used as a vegetable, boiled or cooked in soups. Cornmeal (usually purchased, although a few people still grind their own) is used for cornbread and cornbread dressing, and as a coating for fried seafood. Cajuns still occasionally use cornmeal to make coush-coush, an old-fashioned breakfast food (see below). Cajuns also eat grits—grits with liver, onions, and gravy is a favorite combination—but few eat hominy.

Cajuns used more corn and corn products before commercial rice production provided a widely available and affordable preferred staple. In the early nineteenth century, Robin observed the varied use of corn by south Louisianans:

> The use of corn is universal among the poor and rich. Corn is prepared here in an infinite number of ways. Usually it is ground with wooden mortars and pestles. The white corn is made into flour, and from this can be made a very good mush with either water or milk. The latter, being thicker, is eaten with that type of soup called gumbo. Ordinary corn broken into small grains, like rice, is cooked almost to dryness in a kettle and is called *petit gru*. This nutritious food is quite common. Corn broken into larger grains and cooked with a larger quantity of water is called *sagamite*. . . . Fermented corn flour is boiled and is called *cassant*. Bread is also made of corn, as in Europe. The dough is placed on the fire as soon as it is kneaded. It must be baked in an oven, a dutch oven, or simply on a

leaning board placed close to the fire. . . . For travel, a hard-tack is made of corn . . . there is another type of corn meal, in which the corn is first roasted and during the roasting a little wood ash is added. When the corn and ashes are ground to flour in a mortar the result is called *cold* flour and is especially used as provision on long trips. . . . When it (corn) is green, Negroes, Creoles, and especially the English, eat the roasted ears, which they call dried corn. It is very tender, and the Creoles prepare it in the same way as garden peas (Robin 1966:198–99).

Robin's description gives some idea of the regional corn-related foods to which the Acadian settlers were heir. Some, such as cornbread and grits (gru), are common today. Some contemporary Cajuns still prefer their grits dry-cooked, as Robin described, rather than as gruel. Other corn foods, such as cassant and cold flour, have passed from living memory. Sagamite, a dish not eaten today but remembered, without high regard, by the oldest people in Breaux Bridge, was prepared as Robin described in the early twentieth century. The Native American forerunner of this dish, also called sagamite, consisted of boiled cornmeal with fat and meats or fruit. It was a common food for the colonists (Davis 1959:19). People today do not recall eating this augmented version of the dish.

WHEAT

Wheat flour has always been an imported item in Louisiana. Older people recall that wheat flour was one of the very few products that subsistence farmers had to purchase. Wheat flour is particularly significant to Cajun cuisine because it is necessary for making a roux, a basis of many Cajun dishes. It is also an ingredient in white bread, biscuits, cakes, pastry crusts, pancakes, and some batters used for frying.

VEGETABLES AND FRUITS

All the common, nationally marketed fresh, frozen, dried, and canned vegetables and fruits are available in grocery stores throughout Acadiana. The larger stores, particularly those in urban areas, also carry some novel or uncommon items, such as snow peas, bean sprouts, alfalfa sprouts, and macadamia nuts. As elsewhere in the United States, the availability of vegetables and fruits is no longer a function of local growing seasons and soil types. Virtually all vegetables and fruits are available in some form throughout the year, and some of these are types that have never been grown in Acadiana. Nevertheless, local people prefer *fresh* vegetables and fruits, especially those that traditionally have been grown in their area. Since many families either have gardens or have relatives or friends who have gardens, they do have access to locally grown produce. Even though the consumption of fresh produce is no longer strictly limited by natural seasons, people do tend to eat produce according to the old seasons: okra, corn, and tomatoes are summer vegetables, and mustard greens and cabbage are winter vegetables. Other types of produce commonly grown locally include squashes, beans, sweet potatoes, Irish potatoes, onions, peppers, cucumbers, turnips, eggplant, mirlitons (a type of squash, referred to elsewhere as vegetable pear, chayote, or Aztec pear), melons, pears, figs, strawberries, and pecans. Local people gather and eat wild blackberries and dewberries, and they use wild cherries to make a liqueur known as cherry bounce (see below).

SEASONING VEGETABLES AND HERBS

Seasoning vegetables, often referred to simply as seasonings, constitute a special category of vegetables. Seasoning vegetables are usually not eaten alone or prepared as the main ingredient of a finished dish; rather, they are used to add flavor and texture to other foods. Because they are indispensable parts of so many commonly prepared dishes, seasoning vegetables are probably the vegetables most frequently eaten by Cajuns. Seasoning vegetables include bulb and green onions, red (hot) peppers, parsley, sweet (bell) peppers, garlic, and celery. In Breaux Bridge, onions and red pepper are included in virtually every dish that calls for seasonings, fresh parsley is included in most, and bell pepper is required for many. Breaux Bridge natives are divided in their opinion of garlic: some use it whenever onions are used, some use it only for certain seasoned dishes, and some prefer not to use it at all. Cajuns in southeastern Louisiana use garlic more freely than do those in southwestern Louisiana, perhaps because of the greater Italian influence in southeastern Louisiana. In Breaux Bridge, celery is more dispensable than the other seasoning vegetables. Southeastern Louisianans also use shallots, which are grown commercially along the Mississippi River. Shallots are less commonly used in southwestern Louisiana.

Seasoning vegetables may be purchased at grocery stores or grown in gardens. People express a definite preference for the fresher, home-grown varieties, and even those town and city dwellers who do not maintain full-sized home gardens often grow green onions, parsley, and a pepper plant or two in their flower beds.

Local people insist that red pepper be of the highest quality. They claim that nonlocal brands of red pepper are often lacking in freshness and potency; they prefer local brands of hot sauce and ground red pepper or, better yet, home-grown and home-processed sauces and powders. St. Martin and Iberia parishes constitute the heart of Louisiana's pepper belt, and numerous brands of ground pepper, red hot sauce, green hot sauce, hot relishes, and pickled peppers are produced by local companies. Some of these products are marketed regionally; others, such as the local favorite, Tabasco sauce (the trademarked name for a fermented and aged sauce made only on the Avery Island salt dome in Iberia Parish) are marketed nationally and internationally. Local stores are well stocked with peppers and pepper products, and ground cayenne pepper is available in jars containing more than one pound of pepper. (For a description of Louisiana's pepper industry, see Schweid [1989]).

Despite the diversity and ready availability of regionally produced pepper products, many Cajuns make an effort to acquire home-grown and home-processed pepper products. Some people grow, dry, and grind their own red pepper, usually using the small but potent tabasco pepper or the larger cayenne pepper. Some people also make hot relishes, pickled products, and sauces. Certain individuals are well known locally for their homemade pepper, which they sell or trade informally, sometimes to customers in fairly distant towns.

Cajun cooks in Breaux Bridge rarely use herbs such as basil, marjoram, thyme, rosemary, oregano, and bay leaf in traditional Cajun dishes, although bay leaf is more frequently used than the others, and most of them are used for boiling seafoods. Conversations with Cajuns from southeastern Louisiana suggest that these herbs are more commonly used in that area, as well as in the New Orleans area. Filé powder (powdered sassafras leaves, a legacy of the Choctaw Indians) is a thickener and flavoring agent for some types of gumbo throughout south Louisiana. However, in Breaux Bridge, filé powder is by no means a necessary or even common gumbo ingredient. Some people place a jar of filé powder on the dinner table, so that those who like it can use it. Breaux Bridge natives rarely season an entire pot of gumbo with filé powder.

DAIRY PRODUCTS

In the early nineteenth century, Robin observed the cattle-raising prairie Acadians and noted that they made little use of the dairy products that might have been derived from their herds. "What is even more astonishing to the European is that in the dry season, especially in the winter, milk is a rare thing. The same inhabitants who have several hundred cows go three or four months without a cup of milk" (1966:196). In the 1870s, an observer noted that "with thousands of cows roaming on the prairies, you never see butter or milk in their houses" (Lockett 1969:52). These early observations indicate a relative lack of interest in dairy products among Cajuns that has apparently continued, to a certain degree, into the present. Although Cajuns have traditionally made butter and creamed Creole cheese (see below), they do not have a tradition of making hard cheeses, yogurt, or other dairy products. Today Cajuns do drink milk, use milk in baking, and eat dairy products, such as cheese, ice cream, and yogurt, but these foods are never called typically Cajun. Cajuns do not have a legacy of cooking and eating milk-and-seafood chowders or cream sauces, and no traditional Cajun main dish contains milk, cream, or cheese. Lard and vegetable oil are more commonly used than butter for browning foods. Recently, however, some individuals and some restaurants have begun to combine dairy products with favorite local ingredients to produce new, "gourmet" dishes—sometimes labeled as Cajun—such as crawfish Newburg and seafood/cheese casseroles.

Creamed Creole cheese (or Creole cream cheese) consists of drained, clabbered milk mixed with cream. It resembles yogurt in appearance and texture, but lacks the tart flavor of yogurt. In the past, it was commonly made at home, but today it is marketed in pint tubs by local dairies and by at least one national dairy, which produces it for distribution in south Louisiana and neighboring areas. A newly opened container of creamed Creole cheese has a half-inch layer of cream covering the top of the cheese. People stir the cream into the cheese, add fruit and perhaps sugar, and eat the mixture for breakfast or supper, or as a snack. Older people associate it with the old days, but they point out that today the product is too expensive for frequent use. In local stores, creamed Creole cheese costs about twice as much as yogurt. Fiebleman notes that "Creole cream cheese has proven difficult to make in other parts of the country, possibly because of the absence of certain unidentified but essential bacteria in either the milk or the air" (1971:15).

Sweeteners

Although south Louisiana is a major sugar-producing area, refined sugar and its by-product, molasses, have usually been consumer products for Cajuns. Small farmers could not afford the investment in capital and labor required for refining sugar, so this task was left to the large plantations and sugar cooperatives. In the past refined sugar was one of the very few products that subsistence farmers had to purchase, and cane syrup was the everyday sweetener for Cajun families. Many families grew small patches of sugarcane, which they harvested and took to local sugar millers. Using a horse-powered mill, the miller squeezed the juice from the cane and boiled the juice in an open kettle until syrup was formed. (For a description of Cajun sugar mills, see Post [1962:113–14]). One Acadiana company, Steen's, still makes cane syrup that older people say is "exactly like the kind we had when we were children." Cane syrup was used as a sweetener for baking, and it was poured on breakfast foods, such as coush-coush, sagamite, lost bread (French toast), pancakes, and cracklings. (Cracklings are not always served as "sweet" food; sometimes they are served with cayenne pepper and salt.) Today all the nationally marketed sweeteners, including artificial ones, are used by Cajuns, and cane syrup is no longer the primary sweetener it once was.

Beverages

Of all beverages used by Cajuns today, dark roast coffee is most closely associated with Cajuns and their region. Cajuns drink coffee, usually in small amounts, frequently throughout the day, and some individuals frankly admit that they and others they know are addicted to coffee. Cajuns are very particular about the quality of their coffee, and they claim that their coffee is superior to that of other regions, including New

Orleans. Several people have told me, "You can tell how far you are from south Louisiana by the coffee. The farther away you are, the worse the coffee is." Some also claim that they take their own coffee with them whenever they travel outside south Louisiana.

In the past, women roasted their own coffee beans to the desired dark color, but today people usually buy ground all-purpose, dark roast coffee. By far the most popular brand is Community Coffee, manufactured in Baton Rouge, but numerous other brands, many of them distributed through New Orleans or Houston, are also available locally. Few Cajuns buy the better-known national brands of coffee, and few use coffee with chicory, the New Orleans favorite. (Exceptions to the latter statement are more likely to be found in southeastern Acadiana, which is nearer to New Orleans.)

Cajuns usually prepare coffee by the French drip method, using an enameled French drip pot or a less expensive aluminum drip pot. Hot water is slowly poured over the ground coffee—one tablespoon at a time, according to a folk recipe. Some pots are designed so that the water drips slowly on its own. Coffee is never allowed to boil. To reheat coffee, many people place the coffee pot into a larger saucepan of water, which is then slowly heated, so as to warm the coffee without danger of boiling it. Some people use modern drip coffee makers, such as Mr. Coffee, but few use percolators—an observation that was earlier made by a researcher in the 1930s (Fournet 1939:42). Cajuns describe their coffee as very strong, and outsiders sometimes find it undrinkable. Locals say that coffee should be "strong enough to dissolve the spoon" or "strong enough for the spoon to stand up in the cup."

The offering of coffee to guests is perhaps the most strictly formalized of all Cajun food events: it must be done, and it is virtually always done in the same way. Cajuns of all economic levels own the proper serving utensils. To serve coffee, a serving tray is presented to guests, bearing the necessary number of demitasse cups, tiny coffee spoons, a sugar bowl, and a bowl of nondairy creamer. Sometimes milk or cream is used, but most people prefer nondairy creamer. Often the spoons are hung around the rim of the specially designed sugar or creamer bowl. The host or hostess pours the coffee, and each guest adds the other ingredients to taste. Local people vary in their use of sugar and creamer. Coffee is not necessarily accompanied by sweets or other foods; the coffee is an end in itself.

Beer is another favorite local beverage. Cold beer is the preferred accompaniment to spicy dishes, and many locals, especially men, drink beer with meals, particularly in the evening. Beer is undoubtedly more popular than wine or mixed drinks. The owner of Mulate's, a Breaux Bridge–based restaurant chain, has begun producing Mulate's beer, an amber-colored beer formulated to accompany Cajun food.

As mentioned earlier, Cajuns make a traditional liqueur called cherry bounce. Wild cherries are picked during the summer, placed in jars or bottles, and covered liberally with sugar. After several months, during which the bottles are occasionally turned and opened to release the pressure from fermentation, bourbon, white wine, or vodka is added to the contents. The cherries are left in the bottle, and as the liqueur is consumed, additional bourbon or other liquor is added. The cherries continue to impart their distinctive flavor to the product indefinitely. Cherry bounce takes about six months to mature. Since the Christmas season begins about six months after the wild cherry season, people associate the drinking of cherry bounce with Christmas.

2.

Cajun Cooking

This chapter consists of a series of descriptions of major Cajun dishes. It is not a complete description of all cooked foods eaten by Cajuns (some of which are not labeled as "Cajun"). Nor is it a "food genealogy" describing the historical origins of various dishes, although I occasionally refer to historical origins, especially if these purported origins are part of the folk or popular view of a particular dish. Nor do the following descriptions constitute a complete listing of all dishes which *are* labeled as Cajun. Rather, I list those prepared dishes that are most frequently mentioned and labeled as Cajun when Cajuns discuss and describe their cuisine. The reader will note an emphasis on meat and seafood dishes. Many of the dishes almost always named when Cajuns describe their food are gravy-based meat or seafood main dishes served with rice. Frequently mentioned side dishes often contain meat or seafood and rice as well. In short, Cajun cuisine, as described by both Cajuns and outsiders, centers on seasoned meat and seafood, with rice as the usual accompaniment.

The descriptions of Cajun dishes presented here are not recipes, in the usual sense of the word. Recipes are of limited use in documenting a phenomenon that is judged and appreciated by the relatively "subtle senses of taste and smell" (Gillespie 1979:403). Cajuns rarely prepare their traditional dishes according to written recipes, and they rarely measure ingredients precisely or strictly time the cooking procedures. Rather, they measure ingredients according to the "little of this, little of that" method, and they cook a dish "until it's done." A cook's judgments and actions are based on his or her senses of taste, smell and sight, as are the reactions of those who eat the finished dishes. To better understand the significance of these factors, and to be able to present more than mere recipes for Cajun dishes, I have observed and participated in both the cooking of and the eating of most of the dishes that I describe in this chapter. (A discussion of Cajun cooks and their kitchens is found in chapter 3.)

CAJUN DISHES

ROUX

Many Cajun dishes are based on a roux, made by the browning of white wheat flour. A roux is not a finished dish, nor is it edible by itself; rather, a roux is a temporary product that becomes part of a finished dish. Some locals joke that all Cajun recipes begin with the instruction, "first, you make a roux." To do so, the cook mixes in the pot roughly equal portions of flour and oil (or melted fat) and browns the mixture very slowly, stirring constantly. An insufficiently stirred roux will contain bits of burned and raw flour that will ruin the finished dish. It is impossible to "rush" a roux; often a half-hour or more of the cook's constant attention is required. When the roux reaches the proper color—ranging from a dark chocolate brown for brown gravies, gumbos, and fricassees to "the color peanut butter or a brown paper bag" for more delicate dishes—the cooking process must be stopped abruptly by adding liquid (water or stock) or other ingredients, such as chopped onions (some cooks first refrigerate these to heighten their ability to stop the browning of the flour instantly before it burns). The added liquid combines with the roux to form a relatively thick gravy or sauce; dishes made with a roux necessarily contain more gravy than do similar dishes made without a roux. Although all browning is a painstaking task, the browning of flour to produce a roux is said to be the most difficult of all to master. The ability to make a good roux is the mark of a good cook.

A roux need not be made into a gravy immediately after it is produced. Some cooks make quantities of roux and store the product in jars in the refrigerator. These cooks use the roux as needed, adding it directly to pots of boiling liquid. Regional companies market ready-to-use roux to which a preservative has been added. Local people find this bottled roux to be satisfactory, although it is more expensive than homemade roux.

The browning process does not completely cook the flour component of a roux. Although a roux dissolves in hot liquid a few minutes after the two are combined, locals say that the resulting sauce will not lose its "raw flour" taste until it has been boiled for a long time—a period ranging from an hour to, in extreme cases, an entire day. Cooks taste their sauces periodically to test the degree of doneness of the roux.

RICE AND GRAVY

Rice and brown gravy seasoned with onions is a very common side dish at Cajun meals. Older people say that in the past this dish was always served at the noon meal (dinner), and it was frequently served at the evening meal (supper) as well. A popular cap and tee shirt in Acadiana bear the state seal of Louisiana, but with the words of the state motto, "Union, Justice, Confidence" changed to "Union, Justice, Rice and Gravy." According to a local joke, a Cajun can look at a field of rice and judge how much gravy it would take to cover it.

A basic brown gravy consists of a dark roux to which water has been added. Preferably, the fat used to make the roux should be derived from cooked meat, although other fat or oil will do. Nonfat meat drippings, if available, are added to the gravy, and cooks usually add onions as well. Cooks also add pepper to brown gravy; however, brown gravy is one of the least "peppery" Cajun dishes.

Plain rice is prepared by boiling it in lightly salted water in a closed vessel, until the rice is tender and has absorbed the water. Some cooks remove the rice from the pot after it has partially cooked and steam it until done in a colander over a pot of boiling water. The colander method is also used to reheat leftover rice. Many families today cook rice in automatic rice cookers.

GUMBO

The word *gumbo* has several meanings in Louisiana. The word is thought to be derived from a West African word for okra, and okra is one of its referents in Louisiana. *Gumbo* may also refer to the French Creole language, and to an especially sticky type of mud. However, local people most commonly use the word to refer to a cooked dish that is found throughout south Louisiana. This dish, often described by outsiders as either a thick soup or a thin stew, comes in a wide variety of forms and usually consists of a seasoned mixture of two or more types of meat and/or seafood in a roux-based sauce or gravy. Gumbo is served by ladling it over a dish of rice, or by placing a scoop of rice into a dish of gumbo. People mix the rice and gumbo as they eat. Gumbo with rice is a meal in itself (with bread and drink), although occasionally it is served as one item in a larger meal.

Popular writers and cookbook editors are fond of tracing the origins of Louisiana gumbo in terms of the contributions made to this dish by the various groups of early settlers. (See, for example, Fiebleman [1971:15]; Kane [1949:314]; Mitcham [1978:39]; and Rushton [1979:212].) Fiebleman, whose account is similar to those of other writers, says that the French colonists brought to Louisiana the concept of fish stew, or bouillabaisse. They substituted Louisiana finfish and shellfish for the standard Mediterranean finfish. The Spanish added hot peppers, the Africans added okra, and the Choctaws added filé powder. The Acadians further changed the recipe by dropping finfish as an ingredient. Accounts such as that of Fiebleman have become a part of contemporary popular lore. Several formally educated Cajuns have recited similar accounts to me when discussing gumbo, explaining that "gumbo shows the history of Louisiana and its people." A poem by a local writer, printed on souvenir notecards, recounts the settlement history of south Louisiana in the form of a recipe for "Louisiana Gumbo": "drop in 10 canoes of French explorers . . . Add 17 schooners of Spanish settlers . . . add all the lost and wandering Cajuns . . . thicken the broth with the cream of African tribes . . . stir in a few Texans" (Dillemuth 1974). Stephen Duplantier, a New Orleans native, drew analogies between gumbo and Louisiana geography, geology, and history in his film *Gumbo: The Mysteries of Cajun and Creole Cooking* (1978).

The French traveler C. C. Robin observed in the early nineteenth century that the Acadian settlers in Louisiana ate a dish called gumbo (1966:115). Another traveler who visited Baton Rouge during the same period describes a boardinghouse meal "à la Française":

The table was well covered with different dishes, and a variety of vegetables, among which the most conspicuous, was a large dish of gumbo, served by the hostess at the head, which seemed to be a standing dish, and much in repute, as almost everyone was helped to it. It is made by boiling ocroc [okra] until it is tender, and seasoning it with a little bit of fat bacon. It then becomes so ropy and slimy as to make it difficult with either knife, spoon or fork, to carry it to the mouth, without the plate and mouth being connected by a long string, so that it is a most awkward dish to a stranger, who besides, seldom relishes it, but it is a standing dish among the French Creoles, as much as soup and bouilli is in France (Thwaite 1907:339).

The traveler refers to gumbo as a vegetable, and his description suggests a dish more similar to today's smothered okra, a popular vegetable side dish, than to the more complex okra gumbo. The anonymous "Breaux Manuscript," believed to have been written by a south Louisiana native in the late nineteenth or early twentieth century, contains another lengthy description of a dish called gumbo:

Gumbo is the national dish of Louisianans. . . . It is made from all sorts of meats, fowl, birds, game, fish, etc. cooked on a slow fire in their own juices, with salt, red pepper, and black pepper. The whole is sprinkled with a large amount of dried and powdered sassafras leaves which give an aroma and a certain viscosity to the sauce, much like water in which linseed or macaroni has been steeped. It is hard for a housewife serving *gumbo* to choose pieces swimming in a blackish sauce that leaves them unrecognizable. Her only recourse is to plunge her spoon haphazardly into the homogeneous substance and pour its contents into her guest's plate. The guest then fills the remaining space with a quantity of rice (Ditchy 1966:28).

This passage describes filé gumbo, rather than okra gumbo, and the description applies well to contemporary versions of the dish, which is especially popular in southeastern Louisiana.

Some popular writers insist that gumbo is defined by the fact that it is thickened with okra (which produces a sticky exudate when cooked) or filé powder (Gueymard 1973:14; Mitcham 1978:40). Although this is true of many gumbos, especially those of southeastern Acadiana and New Orleans, it is not true of the most common form of gumbo found in St. Martin Parish and the prairies of southwestern Louisiana. Although many types of gumbo are made in these areas, the favorite is chicken and

pork sausage gumbo (simply called gumbo), which is thickened only by
the roux. Like other Louisiana gumbos, chicken and sausage gumbo is
seasoned with several of the usual seasoning vegetables and herbs—
onions, parsley, and red pepper.

The chicken and sausage gumbo of southwestern Louisiana contains
few ingredients compared to other gumbos found there and elsewhere in
Acadiana. For example, some cooks add bell pepper and celery to the list
of seasoning ingredients for gumbo, and various types of meat and seafood may be included. Cajuns say that any combination of meat and/or
seafood may go into a gumbo. However, in actual practice oysters are the
only seafood commonly combined with meats such as chicken, duck,
squirrel, or rabbit. Sausage, especially andouille (a smoked variety that
does not fall apart when cooked), is an ingredient in most gumbos,
including seafood gumbos. Sometimes ham is used instead of sausage.
Seafood gumbos contain shrimp, crabmeat, and/or oysters, but not finfish. Okra is more likely to be combined with seafood than with meat. In
southeastern Louisiana and in New Orleans, tomatoes may be added to
seafood gumbo. Tomatoes are rarely used in St. Martin Parish, and some
locals say that "gumbo with tomatoes in it is New Orleans gumbo."
Vegetables other than seasoning vegetables, okra, and sometimes tomatoes
are never added to gumbo—gumbo is definitely a meat or seafood soup,
not a vegetable soup. Nor are beef or pork used in gumbo, except in the
form of sausage or ham. If these meats are prepared in a similar manner
and served over rice, the dish is referred to as a stew (see below). However, beef organ meats can be made into a dish sometimes called "cow
gumbo."

The ingredients found in gumbo support the popular local belief that
gumbo is a dish that allows the cook to combine small amounts of various
ingredients, none of which would be sufficient for a family meal, into a
single large dish. A family can take one chicken, combine it with a piece
of sausage, and perhaps add a few oysters, and have a satisfying meal. The
rice "extends" the gumbo, and thrifty cooks add eggs, boiled or poached
in the gumbo, to further extend the dish. Thus, gumbo is an economical
dish, as are many Cajun dishes, because it allows the cook both to feed a
large number of people with a small amount of meat or seafood, and to
use up small amounts of perishable meats or seafoods efficiently. These
functions were probably more important in the past, when Cajun families

were larger, Cajun incomes were lower, and refrigeration was nonexistent.

One dish referred to as gumbo is very different from the others. This is green gumbo (gumbo z'erbe), which is rarely prepared today. Gumbo z'erbe was a meatless Lenten dish made of as many types of greens as were available, including turnip, mustard, spinach, lettuce, and beet tops. These were seasoned with onion, cooked until very soft, and pushed through a sieve. The resulting thick green liquid was not served over rice, though it was often served with rice on the side. Green gumbo has tended to disappear both because it is difficult and time-consuming to prepare and because the removal of church abstinence laws has made meatless dishes unnecessary. In addition, some people say that greens are not a favored Cajun food, and that they ate green gumbo in the past only because they had to.

To prepare a gumbo, the cook browns the sausage, the okra (if any), and the meat (if any) and temporarily removes them from the pot. (Seafood ingredients are not usually browned.) Flour is added to the remaining grease—additional oil or lard is added if necessary—to make a roux, which is stirred and heated until it is dark brown. When the roux reaches the desired color, the cook adds chopped onions and perhaps other seasoning vegetables to the roux. These may be added before the roux is done, if the cook wishes to brown them a bit. The browned meat and okra (if any) are returned to the pot, and the ingredients are covered with water. The pot is allowed to boil, uncovered, until the ingredients are tender to the point of falling apart. Extra water is added when necessary. Salt, red pepper, and perhaps black pepper are also added; the cook judges the proper amount by tasting the gravy. Quick-cooking ingredients, such as oysters, crabmeat, and shrimp, are added near the end of the cooking process, and green onions and parsley are added after these. If filé is used, it is stirred into the gumbo after it has been removed from the heat, since boiled filé causes the gumbo sauce to be undesirably "ropey" or "stringy." Gumbo requires a minimum of three hours' cooking time, and some cooks allow their gumbo to simmer for an entire day.

FRICASSEE (STEW)

A fricassee or stew is similar to gumbo in that it consists of meat or seafood and seasoning vegetables cooked in a dark, roux-based sauce and served over rice. A stew differs from gumbo in that it never contains okra or filé powder, and unlike gumbo it usually contains only one ~~primary~~ meat or seafood ingredient rather than a mixture of meats and/or seafoods.

Sometimes the line between a gumbo and a fricassee is a fine one. For example, locals have difficulty explaining the difference between crawfish gumbo (which does not contain sausage or other meats and seafoods) and crawfish stew. Some people say that the sauce of a stew is thicker than that of gumbo, but the difference is not always apparent to an outsider. Stews do not contain vegetables other than seasoning vegetables, but Irish potatoes can be made into a potato stew, which is served over rice. Common types of stew include chicken, pork, shrimp, crawfish, crab, and game. The small, perishable parts of a freshly butchered cow (the heart, spleen, kidneys, and perhaps part of the liver) were traditionally used to make "cowboy stew" as an on-the-spot meal for the participants in old-fashioned boucheries. Prairie Cajuns of the 1940s referred to this dish as bouillie or cow gumbo (Kane 1943). Older Breaux Bridge residents regret that cowboy stew is not as commonly eaten today as it once was. However, the necessary ingredients—chopped, packaged together, and labeled "mixed debris" or "bouilli" are still sold in local grocery stores.

ETOUFFÉE AND RELATED DISHES

Etouffée—commonly spelled "A-2-fay" on local menus and placards—is a "smothered" dish, that is, one cooked in a closed container. Like a stew, an étouffée contains one primary meat or seafood ingredient and seasoning vegetables, cooked in a sauce or gravy. Unlike stew, an étouffée does not demand a roux; instead, the sauce is derived from a combination of the ingredients' natural juices and water. The dark color of the gravy of most étouffées is achieved by browning the ingredients, scraping the resulting brown particles from the bottom of the pan, and adding water as needed to dissolve these particles into the sauce. An étouffée produces a relatively small amount of gravy, sufficient for adequately moistening and flavoring the rice over which it is served. The cook who desires to extend an étouffée with more than the usual amount of gravy uses a roux and extra water to produce the extra gravy.

Etouffées are made with chicken, pork chops, frog legs, shrimp, crawfish, turkey necks, and turkey tails; many other meats and seafoods are also used. Any vegetable cooked in the same manner is also referred to as an étouffée, as in "greens étouffée." Crawfish étouffée is undoubtedly the most popular of all étouffées. The crawfish fat added to the sauce gives it a distinctive flavor and body. Most crawfish étouffées in Acadiana contain no roux. However, some Breaux Bridge cooks add a light roux, "the color of peanut butter," to extend this dish.

When beef cuts, such as round steak, are prepared in this manner, the dish is referred to as grillades. When redfish, gaspergou, and other large finfish are prepared in this manner, the dish is called courtbouillon. Both grillades and courtbouillon may contain canned tomatoes. In this respect, they are similar to sauce picquante (see below). Grillades and court-bouillon are served over rice.

SAUCE PICQUANTE

Sauce picquante is an extra-peppery stew, served over rice. It is likely to contain canned tomatoes or tomato paste, as well as the usual seasoning vegetables and extra cayenne pepper. It usually contains one primary meat or seafood ingredient. With the exception of chicken sauce picquante, most sauce picquante dishes are made from animals taken directly from the environment: squirrel, rabbit, turtle, frog (including the body flesh as well as the legs), alligator, and wildfowl. The less commonly eaten animals, such as raccoon, nutria, opossum, and muskrat, are likely to be made into sauce picquante. The spicy sauce camouflages the strong, "gamey" flavor of these animals.

JAMBALAYA

Jambalaya resembles the Spanish dish paella, and it may be a descendant of it (Fiebleman 1971:179), although some research points to African origins (Ancelet, Edwards, and Pitre 1991:141). Jambalaya is probably even more variable than gumbo: virtually any combination of meats and seafood may be used, along with the usual seasoning vegetables and ham or sausage. These are browned to produce a gravy. A roux is not normally used, but canned tomatoes or tomato paste may be added to extend and flavor the sauce. About a half-hour before the sauce is done, the cook adds raw or partially cooked rice to the pot. The rice cooks in the sauce, absorbing its flavor and color. The finished product varies in consistency from moist and mushy to dry. It is eaten with a fork rather than with a spoon, and it does not "run" on the plate, unlike étouffées. Jambalaya may be a main dish or a side dish.

RICE DRESSING

Rice dressing is the classic accompaniment to roast beef, roast pork, roast turkey, and fried or roast chicken. It virtually always forms part of Sunday and holiday dinners, and it is often served at other special occasions, such as weddings and club meetings. Rice dressing consists of cooked rice that has been combined with "dressing mix" shortly before serving. Dressing mix is made from ground pork and/or ground beef; ground pork, beef, and/or chicken liver (other organ meats such as beef or pork hearts or chicken gizzards may be added); and ground seasoning vegetables. These are cooked together, with water and perhaps a roux, for hours, until the meat is very tender and the blood from the organ meat has produced a medium-thick gravy. Shortly before serving time, the cook folds the dressing mix into the cooked rice. The resulting dish is light brown, with pieces of meat and seasoning vegetables throughout. It is moist, but not runny, and can be eaten with a fork.

BOUDIN AND OTHER SAUSAGES

Boudin is a soft sausage made of ground pork muscle meat, ground pork organ meat, cooked rice, and seasoning vegetables, all stuffed into a sausage casing made of cleaned hog's intestines. There are two types of boudin: white (boudin blanc) and red (boudin rouge). The more common white boudin is essentially rice dressing stuffed into a sausage casing. Red boudin contains an extra ingredient—pork blood, usually acquired from the wound in the neck of a pig immediately after it is "stuck" with a butcher knife. Health laws prohibit the sale of red boudin, although it is legal to make one's own for personal consumption. Nevertheless, many Cajuns speak of red boudin as if it were illegal under any circumstances.

Boudin was always made at the old-fashioned, work-oriented boucheries, and it is still made at family boucheries. Commercial white boudin is manufactured by local grocery stores, meat packers, and slaughterhouses and sold at grocery stores, convenience stores, and other retail outlets. Cajuns say that boudin is the Cajun fast food. Convenience stores throughout Acadiana advertise hot boudin on their signs and window placards. Since boudin is always eaten warm, these stores have microwave ovens or pots of simmering water for heating boudin. Customers receive their hot boudin wrapped in a piece of paper; because the rubbery skin is said to be inedible, they must suck or squeeze the contents from the casing as they eat. Boudin is a snack food, often accompanied by beer; it is never used as an ingredient in other dishes. So great is its popularity that a local joke defines a Cajun seven-course meal as "a piece of boudin and a six-pack."

Stores in Acadiana sell a great variety of additional types of sausage. These are made of pork, beef, garfish, crawfish, or other meats. Some are smoked; others are not. Some are labeled as having an emphasis on certain seasoning ingredients, as in "extra hot" or "garlic sausage." Homemade venison sausage is popular, and andouille, a sturdy, smoked pork sausage, is preferred for use in long-cooking dishes such as gumbo and jambalaya.

CHAUDIN

Chaudin, also called ponce, is a dish associated with boucheries. To make chaudin, the cook stuffs a cleaned pork stomach with a mixture of ground pork, seasoning vegetables, and perhaps diced sweet potatoes and rice. The stuffed stomach is sewn closed with a needle and thread, browned in grease, and smothered or steamed for several hours in a closed container. As it cooks, the stomach shrinks and compresses the stuffing. Chaudin is sliced and served warm or cold.

BOULETTES

Boulettes or balls are made of virtually any chopped meat or seafood, seasoning vegetables, and cooked rice, bread crumbs, or crumbled corn-bread. These ingredients are combined, sometimes with the addition of a raw egg, and formed into balls or patties. They are stewed in gravy and served over rice, or dredged in flour and deep-fried.

STUFFED CRABS

If a seasoned crabmeat mixture similar to that used for boulettes is pressed into cleaned crab shells and browned in an oven or fried, the dish is called "stuffed crabs."

CRAWFISH BISQUE

If a seasoned crawfish mixture similar to that used for boulettes is stuffed into cleaned crawfish heads, browned, and then added to a roux-based sauce containing crawfish tails, the dish is called "crawfish bisque." Browned stuffed heads are sometimes served as appetizers.

STUFFED VEGETABLES

Squash, mirlitons, or eggplant may be stuffed and served as a main dish. The vegetable is boiled or steamed, cut in half, and partially hollowed out. The material thus removed is combined with browned ground beef or pork, or cooked shrimp and/or crabmeat, along with seasoning vegetables and rice or bread crumbs. This mixture is returned to the hollowed vegetable, which is then baked until brown and tender. Bell pepper is similarly stuffed and baked. Sometimes the seasoned vegetable mixture is baked in a pan rather than in a hollowed-out vegetable.

STUFFED ROASTS

Whole turkeys, whole chickens, beef tongue, and large cuts of beef, pork, venison, alligator, and garfish are "stuffed" before they are roasted or smoked. The cook pierces numerous small holes in the meat and fills each hole with pieces of onion, garlic, and bell pepper, all of which have been dusted with salt and cayenne pepper. Any remaining space in the holes may be filled with additional cayenne pepper. The meat is then roasted, with a small amount of water, in a covered container, either on the stove top or in the oven, or it may be smoked in a storebought or homemade outdoor smoker. Each slice of meat should contain a bit of onion, garlic, and bell pepper.

Some cooks use an alternative method of seasoning large cuts of meat, including whole hogs: using a veterinarian's hypodermic needle, they inject the meat throughout with a mixture of finely powdered cayenne pepper and liquefied seasoning vegetables. A butcher in St. Martin Parish says that he injects the liquid into the veins of the muscle meat, which act as conduits to carry the seasoning to all parts of the meat.

BOILED SEAFOOD

Cajuns boil crawfish, crabs, and shrimp with cayenne pepper and other seasonings. This process is described in detail, using the crawfish as an example, in chapter 5.

FRIED MEATS AND SEAFOODS

Fried shrimp, oysters, finfish, crawfish tails, frog legs, rabbit, and chicken are popular dishes in Acadiana. Breaux Bridge cooks prepare these foods for frying by first liberally dusting them with cayenne pepper, before coating them with batter, cornmeal, flour, or commercial fish-fry. The food is then fried in deep fat. Lard was the traditional fat used for frying, but today cottonseed oil or other vegetable oil is preferred. The resulting crust is peppery throughout and contains pockets of pure cayenne. According to one elderly woman, "that way you catch something good."

The pepper content of fried foods in southeastern Louisiana may be less than what I observed in southwestern Louisiana. However, peppery fried chicken is popular in New Orleans, and a New Orleans-based fast-food chain, Popeye's Fried Chicken, sells "spicy" fried chicken with "Cajun rice" (rice dressing) as a side dish. Popeye's Fried Chicken is popular throughout Acadiana, and the company leases franchises nationally.

BEANS

Cajuns prepare dried beans by boiling them for hours with browned seasoning vegetables and seasoning meats such as sausage, salted pork, pickled pork, ham, or tasso. The beans and seasoning vegetables partially break down to form a thick sauce. Beans served with rice constitute a main dish and a complete meal. Beans, with or without rice, may also be a side dish. White (Navy) beans are a favorite variety in Breaux Bridge. Red (kidney) beans and large lima beans (butterbeans) are also popular.

BREADS

French-style bread loaves were once baked at home for special occasions; the cost did not allow the daily use of wheat flour for bread. However, local bakers have taken over this task—even the oldest residents of Breaux Bridge do not remember when there were no bakeries in town. Today a local bakery supplies consumers with French bread, and regional brands are available in grocery stores. French bread is still regarded as somewhat of a special treat; white sandwich loaves are daily fare. One brand, Evangeline Maid of Lafayette, dominates the market for white, processed bread in southwestern Louisiana. Although stores in Lafayette sell all types of bread, including whole-grain "natural" breads, bagels, and pita, stores in small towns often limit their stock to soft, white breads and a few loaves of light brown bread.

Few people today make homemade wheat bread, although some do bake

breads and cakes as a hobby. However, people commonly make homemade cornbread, which is eaten either with meals or as a snack. Some
people add hot peppers to their cornbread batter, and they occasionally
add cracklings. An old-fashioned breakfast or supper menu includes
cornbread with cracklings, cane syrup, and cold baked sweet potatoes.

COUSH-COUSH

When talking of Cajun food, Breaux Bridge residents frequently mention
coush-coush (or cush-cush), which they characterize as the typical Cajun
breakfast dish of the old days. However, I have never seen coush-coush
prepared, nor have I been told by anyone that he or she has recently eaten
homemade coush-coush. This dish may be talked about more frequently
than it is prepared and eaten nowadays.

Coush-coush is cornmeal batter fried in a small amount of fat. As a
brown crust forms on the bottom of the batter, the cook stirs the mixture,
thus allowing other parts of the batter to brown. This process is continued
until the batter has been transformed into a pan of dry, crisp bits, described as being like sand. People say that coush-coush somewhat resembles dry, packaged breakfast cereals. Like modern breakfast cereals, it is
eaten with milk, sugar (or cane syrup), and fruit or preserves.

DESSERTS AND SWEETS

Cajuns appear to be less interested in desserts than they are in other types
of food. A complete meal need not be followed by a dessert, and most
home-cooked meals I have eaten in Acadiana have not included dessert.
When listing Cajun foods, few Cajuns spontaneously mention desserts;
however, when asked specifically about desserts, they do name certain
ones as typically Cajun. Although virtually all Cajun cooks prepare the
local meat or seafood dishes, a strong interest in baking appears to be
more common among the elderly and among wealthier people—perhaps
because these two groups have more leisure time to devote to baking. The
same cooks who spend a great deal of time and effort in preparing main
dishes according to demanding local aesthetics also praise the taste of various mass-produced, packaged dessert products. I do not wish to imply that
Cajuns do not like their traditional desserts—they do—but I have known
relatively few people to spend their time and effort in making them.

Commonly named local desserts include syrup cake or gateau de sirop (a spice cake made with cane syrup), rice pudding, pecan pie, pecan pralines, bread pudding, fig cake, beignets (fried doughnuts), blackberry dumplings, cream pies with sweet dough crusts, and oreilles de cochon (deep-fried disks of pastry dough, twisted with a fork to produce the characteristic "pig ear" shape, and drizzled with cane syrup before serving). Older locals remember l'estomac de mulatre (mulatto stomach), a ginger cake, as an old-timey confection. They say that in the past oranges served as a special dessert, and cold baked sweet potatoes were the everyday sweet snack.

CAJUN COOKING AESTHETICS

Cajun cookery has three central aesthetic principles: that foods be strongly or intensely flavored; that they be thoroughly cooked; and that they involve certain combinations of ingredients.

STRONG FLAVORS

Cajuns say that meat, seafood, and vegetable dishes should be "highly seasoned" with seasoning vegetables (especially red pepper) and seasoning meats (sausage, ham, salted pork). Coffee should be *strong*; traditional desserts are described as very sweet. One Cajun says that "when you eat Cajun food, you don't have to fantasize about the taste. The taste is obvious." Cajuns assess American food or the food of north Louisiana and Mississippi (southern food) as "bland." They are aware that some outsiders have difficulty in eating their intensely flavored foods. A group of St. Martin Parish residents who were making boudin for a party for an oil-field service company told me that they were using less cayenne pepper than usual, because there would be "a lot of Americans" at the party. A Breaux Bridge woman tells of the consequences of eating Cajun foods for those people who are not used to the local seasonings: "When my father's army buddies visit him, all they do is eat. They gain weight, and they have diarrhea the whole time they're here. That's because they're not used to our rich food. If you grow up here, you have a cast iron stomach." She adds that some mothers put cayenne pepper in their older infants' baby food, "in order to prepare them for table food."

Local people also say that outsiders are taken aback by the strength and flavor of dark roast coffee. "It's funny to watch people who aren't from here when they try to drink the coffee," one person says. "They can't believe how strong it is. They don't want to be rude, so they drink it anyway. It takes time to get used to our coffee, but people can usually learn to like it."

Intensity of flavor is, of course, a subjective experience. One Acadiana journalist, in his book aimed at refuting stereotypes about Cajuns, admits that Cajun food is spicy, but adds that "to refer to it as hot and peppery is just flat wrong" (Angers 1989:70). He and others are concerned about the development of a Cajun food stereotype that simply equates Cajun food with the use of hot pepper, sometimes in absurd ways. For example, a national company sells a "Cajun" beer that contains cayenne pepper, even though there is no precedent for such a combination in Cajun cuisine.

Still, newcomers and visitors almost always describe Cajun food as hot or peppery. Cajuns in southwestern Acadiana say the same, and their frequent assessment of non-Cajun southern cuisine as bland or lacking in pepper implies that they do indeed value the taste of pepper in many foods.

LONG COOKING

Cajun food must be thoroughly cooked, often with the use of moist heat, which allows for long cooking without scorching or drying the food. Some older people point out that in the past, long cooking was needed to kill bacteria and parasites and to tenderize tough meats; but today the preference for lengthy cooking remains even though these concerns are less central. Meats are cooked well past the point necessary to render them edible; meat should be tender enough to slice or pull apart easily and should show no signs of rareness. To achieve this, large cuts of meat are often roasted on top of the stove or in the oven in a covered container with a small amount of water, while other cuts are boiled in seasoned gravy for hours. Meats grilled or smoked over a fire are marinated or basted with sauce or oil, and the seasoning vegetables "stuffed" into meats add extra moisture during the cooking process. Most vegetables are cooked until soft or even mushy. Local people especially dislike lightly steamed vegetables that retain their natural color and crisp texture—much to the frustration of local nutritionists. Dried beans are boiled for hours, until they begin to break down and form a thick sauce. One-pot gravy dishes such as gumbo, fricassee, and étouffée are cooked at high temperatures for hours, until the seasoning vegetables begin to fall apart, thus adding to the thickness of the sauce or gravy. A gumbo with discrete, crisp chunks of onion would be considered inedible. Breaux Bridge natives acknowledge that their food is "cooked to death." They point out that the cook must be willing to invest the time required for such long cooking, claiming that "Cajuns don't go near the stove unless they've got the time to do the job right." A common complaint about outsiders' food is that it is half raw; some local cooks say that many outsiders do not care enough about food to take the time to cook it correctly.

A dish that is sufficiently cooked, by Cajun standards, is likely to demand the process of *browning* at some point in its preparation. The Cajun dishes described earlier illustrate how frequently the process of browning is relevant to both doneness and flavor. Browning in itself does not sufficiently cook food; rather, it is an adjunct cooking method used in combination with other methods, such as boiling, smothering, and roasting. It changes the texture and color of foods in ways that could not be achieved through other methods alone. The crispy flecks of hardening juices and solid ingredients that form on the bottom of the pot during browning dissolve to thicken and darken the sauces. Browning also adds its own distinctive "browned" flavor and thus serves as an additional type of seasoning. The flavor is evident even when the color is not noticeably darker, as with dried beans seasoned with browned sausage and onions. A common criticism of novice cooks is that they do not brown their ingredients dark enough.

COMBINING FOODS

Those main dishes which are most frequently described as Cajun consist of a spicy, multi-ingredient component (meat or seafood plus seasoning vegetables), combined with a relatively bland and simple staple, usually rice. Sometimes the two components are cooked separately and combined upon serving, as is the case with gumbo, étouffée, sauce picquante, grillades, cowboy stew, courtbouillon, dried beans, and fricassee. In other cases, the two components are cooked together or mixed together at some point before serving. This is true of jambalaya, rice dressing, boudin, boulettes, and stuffed vegetables. Cajuns do not eat plain, unadorned rice, nor do they eat gumbo or other sauce-based dishes without rice. Gumbo is not simply a soup that can be poured into a bowl and eaten alone, although some outsiders who are accustomed to eating superficially similar soups without rice sometimes question the logic of adding "unnecessary" calories to what appears to them to be an adequately nourishing bowl of soup.

The serving of these two components—seasoned meat or seafood plus the staple—in sufficient quantities constitutes a complete meal. Thus any sauce-based meat or seafood dish may be, and often is, a meal in itself. Bread is a usual accompaniment to these dishes; it is dipped in the sauce and thus serves as an additional staple, along with the rice. Many Cajun meals include additional side dishes, but the two main components are usually present in some form. For example, a typical Sunday dinner menu includes "stuffed" beef or pork roast (the seasoned meat component), rice dressing and/or rice and gravy (the staple component), plus green peas or smothered green beans, potato salad, and baked sweet potatoes. The ubiquity of and preference for the basic, two-part meal pattern is reflected in the following joke: "A Cajun was visiting New York City. He went into a diner and ordered a hamburger. The waiter asked, 'Will that be with everything?' The Cajun replied, 'No, hold the rice.'"

3.

Cooks and Kitchens

COOKS

It is not surprising that professional Cajun cooks like Paul Prudhomme, Enola Prudhomme, John Folse, and others have become high-profile "ambassadors" of Cajun culture. In Acadiana, cooking is a widely held, often performance-oriented skill, and one that is highly valued in both men and women.

A study conducted in the 1960s of married white homemakers in Evangeline Parish indicated that 95 percent of the women surveyed did the cooking of everyday meals in the home. However, 39 percent of their husbands also cooked domestic meals occasionally, and 9 percent cooked often. In addition, 65 percent of the husbands cooked for special occasions, such as dinners for special guests, holiday meals, and outdoor cooking events (Fontenot 1967:31). These findings are consistent with male and female cooking roles in contemporary Acadiana: women are usually the domestic cooks, men occasionally cook in the home for everyday meals, and men frequently cook for special, public or semipublic occasions, particularly if these involve outdoor cooking—which is usually the case.

The home kitchen is the sphere of the woman of the house, who usually

69

does the grocery shopping, organizes the kitchen, cleans the kitchen, and prepares most family meals. Men and older children sometimes help with all of these tasks; such help is essential if the woman works outside the home. Today's adult women say that they learned to cook from their mothers, grandmothers, or other older relatives, usually female. Older women point out that in their youth, girls began to help their mothers in the kitchen "as soon as we were tall enough to reach the stove." One woman says, "You have to remember that people got married earlier in those days. Some of my friends were married when they were fifteen, and most were married by the age of eighteen. We *had* to learn how to cook." Nevertheless, some women joke about how inept they were in the kitchen when they were newly married, and they point out that learning from older relatives does not stop once a woman is married and in charge of her own home. In addition, many women say that they learned to cook certain versions of some dishes from their mothers-in-law, because their husbands wanted favorite dishes prepared in styles they had grown accustomed to during their childhood.

According to older Cajuns, today's teenage girls are not as domestically oriented as their elders were at the same age. One woman, born in the late 1940s, sees a striking difference between the greater traditional cooking skills of her own generation as teenagers and those of today's teenagers. A local home economics teacher says that a few of her students know how to cook but that many "can't open a can without help." Nevertheless, these young students are eager to learn to cook traditional Cajun dishes, such as gumbo. We may speculate that today's teenagers, unlike those of earlier generations, are not now in a stage of life in which cooking is an important skill, and that these teenagers may well seek out their elders' advice, as well as advice from home economics classes and cookbooks, when they are older.

As pointed out earlier, some Cajun men occasionally prepare family meals. Like their wives, these men enjoy cooking and take pride in their skills; there is no stigma attached to a man who cooks in the home. However, men's cooking usually is associated with special occasions, most of which are outdoor events that include a larger number of guests than does an everyday meal or an average Sunday dinner for the extended family. Because these events include large numbers of people, men frequently cook in much larger quantities than women do. Men usually cook in full view of the guests, too, so that watching the cook becomes part of the entertainment. Thus, men's cooking is more likely than women's cooking to be public or semipublic in nature.

Cajun men originally learned how to cook out of necessity. The traditional subsistence-based occupations, with the exception of farming, required that men spend long periods of time away from home, in the marshes, the swamps, and on boats in the coastal waters. "Being Cajun, we weren't willing to go for even one day without a good meal," one man notes. Today, Cajun men and boys learn to cook from other men, often while on hunting or fishing expeditions. As one explains, "When a group of us goes hunting, we eat something we kill that day. If we're squirrel hunting, we skin and clean some of the squirrels at the camp, and somebody makes a squirrel sauce picquante. Usually each man is known for being the best at cooking a particular food, and each man cooks what he's best at. Camp food is the best, because you get the freshest meat, and you have the experts to cook it." Men and boys also learn to cook at the public and semipublic food events at which men are the primary cooks. These include crawfish and seafood boils, family boucheries, and community festivals. For example, at one crab boil I attended, a grandfather and his eight-year-old grandson cooked the second batch of crabs, while the attention of the other guests was devoted to eating rather than to watching the cooking process. At events where men cook, male guests gravitate toward the cooking site, to watch, to advise, and to discuss and compare cooking techniques.

A male cook is likely to concentrate his efforts on meat or seafood main dishes. Items acquired directly from the environment, such as game or fresh fish, are strongly associated with men's cooking. The less commonly eaten varieties of animals are sometimes called men's foods or camp foods (foods eaten at hunting or fishing camps). A middle-aged Cajun woman comments, "When men go to their own hunting camps—the kind you can get to only by boat, not the family camps—they eat some disgusting foods: raccoon, nutria, muskrat, 'possum, alligator. They'll eat anything. I would never serve those foods to my family; I would never allow them in the house." Several other women were present when this statement was made. All agreed that these foods are indeed men's foods or camp foods, but about a third of the women present disagreed with the speaker's evaluation of these foods, saying that these foods are good if properly prepared, and that there is no reason to bar them from the family kitchen.

In addition, barbecue is always prepared by men. The term *barbecue* refers to any food that is cooked outdoors over a fire, on a grill, or in a smoker; it does not refer to the use of a special barbecue sauce, although a sauce or marinade may be used. Boiling crustaceans and roasting pigs are also men's work, and these tasks, too, are done outdoors. When men cook foods that are also frequently cooked by women for ordinary domestic meals (for example, gumbo, sauce picquante, jambalaya, or fried fish), they commonly prepare these outdoors as well. Since men often cook these dishes in large quantities for numerous guests, they are likely to use an outdoor cooking site, where there is more room for the large pots than there is on a kitchen stove.

Cajun male cooks are performers: they cook in front of an audience. At food events at which men cook, the guests arrive before or during the cooking process. The cook is the center of attention and obviously enjoys the comments, queries, and compliments he receives from onlookers. One Cajun man explains the significance of public or semipublic cooking to Cajun men: "Cajun men like to be the providers, for their families and for other people who are guests on their territory. They like to show you that they are self-sufficient—even the ones who work at desk jobs all week. They like to be good hosts, and they like to show you what they can do."

Cajun women say they are glad that men cook, because their cooking is good, and it results in a break from kitchen work for women. Some women say that men "show off" when they cook, and they point out that male cooking does not necessarily result in a holiday for women. As one woman says, "When my husband cooks—and he loves to cook—he only does the fun part, the showy part. He won't chop the onions—I have to do that for him—but he'll stand there for hours, stirring and stirring, while his friends watch. It's a real show when he serves his gumbo, but he won't wash the dishes afterwards." Another woman notes that Cajun men seldom experience the drudgery of having to cook day after day: "Sure, Cajun men are good cooks. They should be. They cook what they want, when they want, and they don't burn the food because they have to answer the telephone or take care of the kids or have a hundred other interruptions."

KITCHENS

All Cajun homes have indoor kitchens, and many homes have outdoor kitchens or cooking sites as well. The size and layout of indoor kitchens and the type of equipment found in them vary with the age of the houses and the income and personal preference of the owners, but virtually all indoor kitchens in Cajun homes in Breaux Bridge and elsewhere have modern gas or electric stoves and ovens, refrigerators, and hot and cold running water. Older residents recall that such was not the case in many homes before World War II, when kerosene or wood stoves were not uncommon, and refrigerators and running water were luxuries beyond the reach of some. An appliance dealer who moved to Breaux Bridge shortly after World War II says that the late 1940s and 1950s were busy years for appliance salesmen throughout Acadiana, because many people were then beginning to modernize their kitchens. Today, those residents with comfortable incomes equip their kitchens with the highest quality appliances they can afford, including dishwashers, garbage disposals, trash compactors, deep freezers, and microwave ovens.

A Cajun home often has some sort of outdoor cooking site. It may be an area of the yard where a barbecue grill or butane burner and picnic tables are set up for special occasions, or it may be a permanent, brick-floored, and perhaps covered patio. Some homes have elaborate, completely functional second kitchens. These are called outdoor kitchens (even if completely enclosed) or men's kitchens. A man who lives in the countryside near Lafayette explains, "As soon as a man can afford it, he builds himself his own kitchen. I've seen it done all over the region. He builds it himself and usually attaches it to the back of the house. Some are screened in; some are made of wood or brick, with large windows that are opened in the summertime. Men usually furnish their kitchens with surplus military stoves or used restaurant or industrial equipment. Cajun men are very proud of their kitchens—this is where they are the hosts and the entertainers." These kitchens vary in size and complexity, but there is an emphasis on practicality and function—reflected, for example, in the choice of durable institutional appliances over more decorative types. Men's kitchens are furnished with large stoves, refrigerators, and sinks, and ample counter space. Some have deep freezers, fish-cleaning tables with drains, coolers for beer kegs, institutional deep-fat fryers, ceiling fans, bug electrocutors, and special equipment for boiling seafood or roasting or smoking large cuts of meat.

The indoor kitchen is relatively private; this is where meals are cooked for family members and a few guests. The outdoor kitchen or cooking site, on the other hand, is relatively public. It is here that men cook for special occasions, which usually include large numbers of guests. Here, also, men carry out certain types of cooking and food-related activities that would be impractical to do indoors: boiling seafood, opening oysters, cleaning fish and game, roasting hogs, and cooking very large quantities of any type of food.

Community kitchens are common throughout Acadiana. These are located in public or semipublic buildings, such as veterans' halls, church or town community centers, school cafeterias, Knights of Columbus halls, and National Guard armories. Community kitchens are furnished with institutional equipment. Residents rent or "borrow" these halls for special events, such as wedding receptions and club meetings, and they use the kitchens to prepare food for these events. In some cases, such as that of Breaux Bridge Veterans' Home, local cooks employed by the facility serve as caterers for most events held at the hall.

EQUIPMENT

Local opinion holds that two types of cooking vessels are superior to all others: cast iron and Magnalite. Cast-iron pots and pans were the old-fashioned, traditional cooking vessels, and people continue to use them today. However, the extra-heavy cast-aluminum cookware manufactured by the Magnalite company is in common use today. Both cast iron and Magnalite are durable and heavy enough to allow the slow, even heating necessary for browning flour and other ingredients, but people prefer Magnalite, despite its higher price, because it does not need to be seasoned, and it does not rust. Some people use surplus military cookware, which is similar to Magnalite.

The preference for modern Magnalite cookware over traditional cast-iron cookware reflects the general attitude toward modern conveniences. Local people eagerly adopt technological innovations, if these do not adversely affect the quality of the finished dish. For example, automatic rice cookers are extremely popular. A Lafayette department store manager says that automatic rice cookers are among the fastest-selling items in the store. The relatively few Breaux Bridge residents who have food processors praise these machines, which greatly aid in the almost daily chore of chopping seasoning vegetables. These residents are divided in their opinion of another time-saver, the microwave oven. Microwave ovens are common in the homes of those who can afford them, Cajun microwave cookbooks are available, and appliance stores in Lafayette offer free demonstrations and short courses in Cajun microwave cookery for prospective customers. Some people like their microwave ovens and use them frequently; others say they are disappointed by these appliances. Those whose microwave ovens sit idle say they can readily tell the difference between foods cooked in a microwave oven and foods cooked by conventional methods.

Innovations in cooking equipment are not limited to those made available by mass marketing. Some Cajun men invent and build their own specialized cooking equipment, using skills learned in the oil fields, such as metal cutting and welding. For example, a man may make an outdoor grill or smoker by cutting an oil drum in half vertically, hingeing the two halves together to form a stable lower section and a moveable upper lid, adding a grill and a handle, and mounting the apparatus on a heavy metal pipe attached to a metal or cement base. Small versions of these grills are found in people's yards, while larger versions, made from drums that are about twelve feet long and four feet in diameter, are mounted on wheels and used at community fairs and festivals. A self-proclaimed "barbecue expert" who supplements his income by cooking at regional festivals and other special events claims that his homemade grill is the largest in the world. It is permanently mounted on a flatbed truck. Men also construct outdoor smokers, which they call "Cajun microwaves," by cutting and welding together pieces of industrial sheet metal.

Local cooks have found a variety of solutions to the problems inherent in suspending and turning a whole hog over a fire. They may encase the pig in a tight cage or box made of chicken wire, and vertically suspend it over the fire with a chain. The chain is connected to a power source—perhaps a modified lawn mower motor—which causes the chain and the pig to spin. Some people mount the wire-encased pig on a homemade, horizontal rotisserie, which is turned by hand or by a power source. In either case, the roasting pig and the fire are partially surrounded by a "tent" of sheet metal, which protects the fire from the wind and reflects heat back onto the pig. One man says that some cooks construct a metal box, "like a coffin," place the pig inside, and bury the box in the coals. In order to learn about innovations in hog-roasting technology, several Breaux Bridge residents have made trips to the Marksville/Mansura area of Avoyelles Parish, the home territory of the "best" hog-roasters. The Marksville/Mansura residents were reputedly the originators of the roasting "coffin," and the first cooks to inject seasonings into meat with a hypodermic needle, as described in chapter 2.

4.

Cajuns and Crawfish

The crawfish is the dominant food-related ethnic symbol in Acadiana. It is arguable that the crawfish is the most important of all Cajun ethnic symbols today. Its use as a symbol is ubiquitous, and it is acceptable as an ethnic emblem to a wide variety of Cajuns. Revon Reed, a Cajun teacher, writer, and radio personality who has long been active in the Cajun ethnic revival, has predicted that "anthropologists of the future" will classify the crawfish as the symbol of Cajuns in the twentieth century (R. Reed 1976:109; see also Gutierrez 1984).

Why is the crawfish so popular and effective as an ethnic symbol? What messages does it communicate? The interpretation of the crawfish as symbol can help us understand why Cajun food in general is so important as an expression of ethnic identity.

In contemporary Acadiana, the image of the crawfish is frequently associated with the expression of ethnic/regional consciousness and pride. For example, a popular license plate, bumper sticker, tee shirt, and hat show an upraised fist holding a crawfish, with the accompanying slogan, "Cajun Power." The terms *Cajun, Acadian, Cajun Country,* and *Louisiana* often appear in conjunction with crawfish imagery in tourist-oriented advertisements and on souvenirs. There are crawfish key chains, combs, plates, and plaques; mechanical toy crawfish; seesaw-riding crawfish en-

cased in fluid-filled plastic domes; and locally produced children's books
that feature crawfish characters. Available in St. Martin Parish are preserved (real) crawfish attached to plaques or sitting in miniature crawfish
nets—the products of a local cottage industry. Advertisements aimed at
tourists and convention planners feature crawfish. Local jewelers sell
expensive gold or silver crawfish pendants and earrings, and clothing
stores sell crawfish logo shirts.

For years an outdoor mural in downtown Lafayette had as its focus a
giant crawfish holding an oil rig in one claw, surrounded by pictures of
other items commonly associated with Cajuns—the flag of Acadiana, an
Acadian cottage, a horse race. The University of Southwestern Louisiana
sponsored a contest for the design of a new icon for the Ragin' Cajuns in
the early 1980s. The school did not specifically solicit crawfish imagery,
but the winning design portrays a Ragin' Cajun astride a bucking
crawfish, and the second prize was awarded to a stylized representation of
a crawfish.

The examples of crawfish symbolism described here are modern ones,
proliferated by the regional media and mass marketing. There are no
indications in historical sources, oral folklore, or oral history that the
crawfish was a recognized symbol of ethnicity for Cajuns in earlier times.
However, it does appear that Cajuns were associated with the crawfish by
both Cajuns and non-Cajuns before the advent of commercialized
crawfish iconography. A popular summary of crawfish "legendry," sold
locally as a souvenir in the 1970s, states that "when a bayou baby is nine
days old, his mother sticks his finger in a crawfish hole, and that makes
him a Cajun" (L. Guirard 1973). In the early 1940s, a similar motif was
found in a "taunting jingle flung at Cajun youngsters by Negro children," collected by field workers for the Louisiana Writers' Project of the
WPA (Saxon, Dreyer, and Tallant 1945:200):

> Frenchman! Frenchman! Nine days old!
> Wrung his hand off in a crayfish hole.
>
> Frenchman! Frenchman! Nine days old,
> Got his hand broke off in a crayfish hole.

A longer version of a similar song, entitled "Cribisse! Cribisse!"
("Crawfish! Crawfish") was collected in French Creole in the 1930s
(Whitfield 1939:138). In Whitfield's English translation, it runs:

Crawfish, crawfish, got no show, baby,
Crawfish, crawfish, got no show,
The Frenchman ketch 'im fer to make gumbo, baby.

Get up in the morning you find me gone, baby,
Get up in the morning you find me gone,
I'm on my way to the crawfish pond, baby.

Frenchman, Frenchman, only nine days old, baby,
Frenchman, Frenchman, only nine days old,
Broke his arm in a crawfish hole, baby.

Crawfish ain't skeered of a six-mule team, baby,
Crawfish ain't skeered of a six-mule team,
But run from a Frenchman time he see 'im, baby.

Look all 'round a Frenchman's bed, baby,
Look all 'round a Frenchman's bed,
You don' find nothin' but crawfish heads, baby.

One contemporary Cajun ethnic joke told by Cajuns draws on a theme similar to that of verse four above: a mother crawfish calms her offsprings' fears of horses and cows, but tells them to run away quickly when they see a Cajun, because "he'll eat anything."

Such songs and jokes mildly ridicule Cajuns for their excessive love of crawfish and for their unconventional eating habits. These examples associate Cajuns with crawfish, but the association is not a particularly positive one from the Cajun point of view. Elderly residents of Breaux Bridge confirm that in their youths the crawfish was a low-status food—and not a symbol of Cajun pride. There was little tourist demand for them, although traveling gourmets did seek out crawfish at such places as the Hebert Hotel restaurant in Breaux Bridge as early as the 1920s. Local people recall that crawfish were so plentiful that hordes of them migrating across roads commonly created traffic hazards (something that still happens occasionally), and housewives in low-lying areas could scoop up a bucketful for dinner from their own back yards. Crawfish were "poor people's food," provided freely by the swamps and streams.

Cajuns who lived on the edge of the Atchafalaya Basin in the 1930s said that crawfish were "just another variety of fish," and that they became tired of eating them so often; these Cajuns sometimes made financial sacrifices to be able to purchase canned salmon (Jacobi 1937:29–30).

Like other aspects of traditional Cajun culture, crawfish eating was ridiculed by twentieth-century newcomers, who frequently did not recognize the animal as an acceptable food item. Cajuns were accused of eating what outsiders perceived as unclean, inedible vermin. Both outsiders and some Cajuns associated crawfish eating with isolated, "backwards," swamp-dwelling Cajuns.

The eating of crawfish, like other aspects of Cajun culture, has since undergone a change in status. Like being Cajun, eating crawfish is no longer something to be ashamed of, and crawfish are no longer "poor people's food." By 1958 the esteem for crawfish had risen to the point that the town of Breaux Bridge could be "honored" by being named the Crawfish Capital of the World. It is noteworthy that while crawfish are praised by the town's historic marker, erected in 1959, Cajuns themselves are not mentioned. The state legislature honored crawfish nine years before it created CODOFIL and named the region Acadiana.

Today the crawfish is an expensive food item, and one that serves as a gourmet food in some contexts. An elderly Breaux Bridge woman says, "Now the big shots eat crawfish, and the poor can't afford to. I wish I had eaten more back then; now I can't afford to buy them." Actually, able-bodied Cajuns with low incomes can still catch crawfish, even if they cannot afford to buy them.

The change in status of the crawfish as food is illustrated by a story told in Breaux Bridge about an old crawfisherman who used to take the long way home with his catch from the Atchafalaya swamp in order to avoid the humiliation of being seen with crawfish by the Lafayette "city folk" picnicking on the levee. Today, he still must take the long way home in order to avoid the city folk, who now deluge him with offers to buy his crawfish.

When and how did the crawfish become a widespread and widely recognized emblem of Cajun ethnicity? Locals say that modern, commercialized crawfish iconography was not common before 1960, and that it became increasingly popular during the 1970s. No one knows who first designed crawfish "Cajun Power" tee shirts and bumper stickers, or who first discovered that plastic combs shaped like lobsters could be ordered from novelty companies with the words "State of Maine" replaced by the words "Cajun Louisiana." However, it is known that local Cajuns designed and produced keepsakes with the crawfish emblem for the 1959

Breaux Bridge Centennial Celebration. These were intended as much for townspeople as for tourists. That year Breaux Bridge merchants distributed wooden nickels with crawfish imprinted on one side, and several other crawfish trinkets were available. A town flag was also created: its centerpiece is a crawfish, surrounded by other symbols of Cajuns and/or the community. At that time, the specific association between crawfish and the Cajun ethnic group—as opposed to the community of Breaux Bridge—was not as overt as it later became. In 1960, the Centennial Celebration was replaced by the Crawfish Festival, which prompted the further proliferation of the crawfish as an emblem in the Breaux Bridge area.

It is understandable that the crawfish should have become a symbol of Breaux Bridge and St. Martin Parish. Throughout south Louisiana, communities sponsor festivals that focus on a local product, usually a food. For example, there is the Rice Festival in Crowley, Yam Festival in Opelousas, Sugar Festival in New Iberia, Alligator Festival in Franklin, Boudin Festival in Broussard, Oyster Festival in Galliano, Frog Festival in Rayne, Cotton Festival in Ville Platte, and the Shrimp and Petroleum Festival in Morgan City. The crawfish has long been a major product of St. Martin Parish, making it a logical choice as a festival theme for Breaux Bridge.

Today, however, the crawfish has become a symbol for all Cajuns, and not just those who live in major crawfish industry areas. Some of the other festivals' products occasionally serve as Cajun ethnic emblems, but none as often as the crawfish. The Breaux Bridge Crawfish Festival itself is partly responsible for calling attention to the crawfish as a Cajun symbol. The festival has always been immensely popular among Cajuns throughout the region as well as among tourists. Cajuns from elsewhere in Acadiana may first have seen the crawfish used as an emblem at the Breaux Bridge festival, or they may have become aware of it through media attention to the festival—including national media coverage (Esman 1981:92).

The growth of the Crawfish Festival coincided with other developments. Stirrings of a Cajun ethnic revival had already begun by 1960. During the 1950s, Cajuns' income, education, and self-esteem were beginning to rise, and in 1955 the bicentennial of the Acadian exile was celebrated in some parts of Acadiana. By 1960 being Cajun was, for some

Cajuns at least, an acceptable identity, and one that could be expressed openly through public symbols. The crawfish was one of several available symbols, and the success of the Crawfish Festival focused attention on it (Esman 1981:179–80). In addition, the crawfish was becoming economically significant throughout Acadiana. Crawfishing as an economic enterprise had been a seasonal activity limited chiefly to the Atchafalaya Basin and other swamp areas. In 1959 modern, commercial crawfish farming began, a practice that has allowed greater numbers of Cajuns throughout much of Acadiana to participate in the crawfish industry as farmers, marketers, and restaurant owners. The Breaux Bridge festival contributed to the growth of the industry: after the centennial celebration faced a shortage of crawfish, a local politician helped obtain a state grant to fund crawfish farming in St. Martin Parish. The festival also spurred outsiders' interest in the crawfish as food, and this in turn was an economic boon to the crawfish industry, the restaurant industry, and the regional tourist industry.

The rise in status of the crawfish as food and the modern expansion of the crawfish industry partly explain the crawfish's acceptance as an ethnic emblem, while the existence of the Crawfish Festival and the influence of mass media and mass marketing in Acadiana partly explain its proliferation. However, these factors do not completely explain the widespread acceptance of the crawfish as the symbol of Cajuns. Both the French language and the Coonass image have been offered as competing ethnic symbols. Both, like the crawfish, have undergone changes in status and have been proliferated in part through the mass media and mass marketing. Yet each has been found unacceptable by some Cajuns. So why is the crawfish a widely accepted, successful ethnic symbol?

The power of the crawfish as an ethnic symbol is enhanced by its dual role as a food (a part of culture) and an animal (a part of nature). Because it is both, it possesses a broad range and flexibility as an ethnic symbol. It is what anthropologist Victor Turner calls a "multivocalic" symbol, one "susceptible of many meanings" (1969:8). It is also a very practical symbol in the contemporary setting. The following chapters explain the significance of the crawfish as food and as animal—a distinction that is not always clear-cut.

5

Catching, Cooking,
and Eating Crawfish

Unlike the Anglo-Americans who settled in much of the southern United States, the French who settled in south Louisiana brought with them to the New World a tradition of eating crawfish, which were also eaten by the local Indians (Comeaux 1972:63–65). By the time the Acadian refugees began to arrive in Louisiana, crawfish were important enough to the colonists that they took steps to ensure a ready supply. A military officer who traveled in Louisiana before 1770 observed that "The crawfish abound in this country; they are in every part of the earth, and when the inhabitants chuse a dish of them, they send to their gardens, where they have a small pond dug for that purpose, and are sure of getting as many as they have occasion for" (Pittman 1973:5). Another observer of the same period noted that the colonists also caught wild crawfish: "The whole levee part of the river abounds in crayfish. Upon my first arrival in the colony, the ground was covered with little hillocks, about six or seven inches high, which the crayfish had made for taking the air out of the water, but since dikes have been raised for keeping off the river from the low grounds, they no longer show themselves. Whenever they are wanted, they fish for them with the leg of a frog, and in a few moments they will catch a large dish of them" (Le Page Du Pratz 1774:277). Thus the Acadian refugees entered a physical environment in which crawfish were plentiful, and a social environment in which methods for procuring crawfish were known to local inhabitants, among whom the crawfish was an accepted and common food item. Although we do not know the details of the early Acadian settlers' first encounters with the abundance of Louisiana crawfish, there is no reason to presume that they avoided crawfish as food. Those Acadian farmers who moved into the swamps during the nineteenth century probably increased their crawfish consumption, as hunting and gathering activities came to take precedence over agriculture (Comeaux 1972:17–21). By the late 1880s there was a small but established commercial crawfish industry within market distance of New Orleans, and in the 1920s commercial exploitation of crawfish in the Atchafalaya Basin began (Comeaux 1972:64).

THE CRAWFISH INDUSTRY

For over two centuries Cajuns have lived in a region that is one of the world's most productive sources of crawfish. Each year between December and May the streams, ponds, swamps, and ditches of south Louisiana yield an abundance of crawfish. The Atchafalaya Basin swamp is the primary source of wild or deep-water crawfish, and crawfish farms greatly add to the region's commercial crop. Over 80 percent of the world's supply of commercial freshwater crawfish come from Louisiana, and the state is the world leader in crawfish cultivation (Huner 1990; 1991). Figures compiled by the Louisiana Seafood Promotion and Marketing Board (n.d.) show healthy growth in the crawfish industry during the 1980s. By 1987 there were 135,000 acres of crawfish ponds, up from 50,000 acres in the late 1970s. Louisiana's 3,000 crawfish farms, mostly located in Acadiana, account for over 90 percent of the nation's crawfish pond acreage. In 1978 the combined commercial harvest of wild and pond-raised crawfish was 45 million pounds (McSherry 1982:8). By 1987 the combined harvest had grown to 100 million pounds, nearly three-quarters of which was pond-raised. In 1987 the crop was worth 37 million dollars, the industry employed 15,000 people, and its estimated annual economic impact on the state was 135 million dollars.[1] No one has

---

1. Unless otherwise noted, the source of data on the crawfish industry in this paragraph is The Louisiana Seafood Promotion and Marketing Board.

made a reliable estimate of the amount of additional crawfish caught and eaten by noncommercial, Sunday crawfishermen, who scour roadside ditches and swampy areas for personal consumption.

Both the major natural crawfish-producing areas and most of the commercial crawfish ponds are located in Cajun parishes, and Cajuns dominate these industries. The fishermen who work in the Atchafalaya Basin catch wild crawfish in homemade traps (see Comeaux [1972]; G. Guirard [1989]). They sell their catch directly to friends or other customers from roadside trucks, or else to local distributors of various types (processing plants, wholesale dealers, restaurants, seafood markets), who resell the crawfish, live or processed, to the public or to other distributors. The fishermen commute by boat to fishing areas in the swamp from towns on the edge of the Atchafalaya Basin. These towns serve as initial processing and distribution centers.

Most of the region's early processing plants, which were also wholesale and retail dealerships, were located in St. Martin Parish, on the western fringes of the basin, and in Assumption and Iberville parishes, on the eastern fringes of the basin (Carroll and Blades 1974:1). Their swampside location was once the most logical place to build a processing plant. But with the expansion of crawfish farming and the increased use of trucking by the industry, the number of plants multiplied and spread to other areas of Acadiana. By 1991 the plants in the immediate vicinity of the basin made up about one-third of the 117 processors listed in the Louisiana Crawfish Processors Directory.

Initially, most of the region's commercial crawfish farms were located west of the Atchafalaya Basin, with their greatest concentration in the rice-producing western prairies, where flooded rice fields serve as crawfish ponds during the off season for rice. Today commercial crawfish ponds can be found in low-lying areas throughout much of Acadiana. Crawfish farming is a modern endeavor that requires knowledge of aquaculture management and technology. Crawfish farmers often belong to the Louisiana Crawfish Farmers' Association, the Louisiana Aquaculture Association, and other trade organizations, through which they keep up to date on the latest scientific and marketing research conducted by various state and federal agencies and by the region's universities. Trade organizations sponsor seminars, journals, and newsletters about innovations in crawfish farming and marketing. Crawfish farmers can seek advice about building and managing ponds from the Crawfish Research Center at the University of Southwestern Louisiana, and from the U.S. Soil Conservation Service, the Cooperative Extension Service, and the National Sea Grant Program (Huner and Romaire 1990:21).

Crawfish farmers sell their crop to wholesalers, seafood markets, or restaurants. Some own restaurants or markets in conjunction with their farming business. They also truck their crawfish to the same processing plants to which traditional fishermen sell their crawfish catches. In addition, farmers sometimes harvest their ponds by opening them to the public. Television commercials invite people to bring their families, crawfish nets, ice chests, and picnic lunches to the ponds for a day of crawfishing and relaxation. For the crawfish they harvest themselves, the customers pay a lower price than they would pay at a retail outlet—and the farmer saves on the high cost of harvesting.

Live crawfish arrive at processing plants and other distribution centers in burlap or plastic produce sacks containing approximately forty pounds each. Crawfish must be kept alive until they are cooked, and handlers of crawfish at all points of the distribution chain take care that the animals are not crushed or overheated. They must be packed tightly in the sacks; otherwise they will attack and injure each other. Properly handled crawfish can remain alive in sacks for three or four days. Processing plants often resell much of the live crawfish, still in forty-pound sacks, to restaurants, retail stores, or consumers.

The remainder are processed. Some are boiled and sold as a ready-to-serve product to other distributors or consumers. Others are partially cooked (steamed or parboiled), after which workers, usually women, peel the crawfish, separating the edible tail meat from the inedible head, thorax, and tail shell. This work is done by hand. Since payment to workers is made according to the amount of tail meat produced, speed and dexterity are desirable. The tail meat is sealed in plastic bags, usually containing one pound each, and either chilled for quick sale or frozen for off-season sale. Bags of crawfish that are marketed locally in retail outlets are sold with a small plastic container of orange or yellowish crawfish "fat" (actually the animal's liver). Cajuns consider the flavorful fat to be indispensable in most crawfish dishes, and they say that crawfish with ample fat are superior. Fat is usually evident in the crawfish at the point where its tail is broken from its body; processing-plant workers save this fat in containers as they peel the tail meat. Parboiled tail meat must be further cooked before it is eaten.

Many plants now sell frozen whole crawfish, cooked or uncooked, and frozen tail meat from which the fat has been washed to improve shelf life. A few plants sell frozen cooked crawfish entrees, or frozen large crawfish boiled in salty, dill-flavored water for the Scandinavian market (Huner 1990:45). Soft-shelled crawfish, a new aquaculture product, are raised in tanks and harvested shortly after they molt. Most are sold frozen, sometimes stuffed with seafood dressing and breaded (Huner 1990:46).

Local people may catch their own crawfish directly from local waters with specially designed crawfish nets. They may use beef melt (spleen) or fish heads for bait. People also catch crawfish with baited strings and dip nets. Noncommercial fishermen do not usually use the commercial fishermen's large traps, which must be left overnight.

Louisiana consumers today usually purchase rather than catch their live crawfish. Live crawfish are available at processing plants and seafood markets, and from local fishermen. Boiled crawfish are sold at processing plants, seafood markets, restaurants, and some grocery stores. Peeled tail meat is sold at seafood markets and grocery stores, or it may be purchased cooked, as part of various dishes, at local restaurants or from local, nonprofessional cooks who are known for their skills with certain dishes within a community.

Most of Louisiana's commercial crawfish harvest is consumed in south Louisiana, including New Orleans. Most of the remainder is sold within a day's trucking distance of Louisiana. Texas is the biggest crawfish market outside of Louisiana (Louisiana Crawfish Promotion and Research Board 1991.) Shipping difficulties and lack of demand have thus far precluded the widespread marketing of live crawfish throughout the United States. Market analysts know that sales of live crawfish are likely to remain low among people outside the Louisiana area who do not know how to cook live crawfish, even if the shipping difficulties were solved. Therefore, efforts to expand the crawfish market concentrate on peeled tail meat, which is more likely to be adopted as a food by people who are not yet familiar with crawfish.

BOILED CRAWFISH AND CRAWFISH BOILS

The dish known as boiled crawfish—crawfish that have been boiled alive and served unpeeled—is probably the most popular crawfish dish among Cajuns. Until the advent of commercially processed, semi-cooked crawfish, the boiling of live crawfish was a necessary stage in the preparation of every crawfish meal in the home. Today boiling (or partial boiling) of live crawfish may be done at a processing plant, but it is still the initial and necessary step that transforms the animal into a food, although many additional steps may be taken to produce certain elaborate crawfish dishes. The crawfish boil is not the only food event at which crawfish are eaten, but it is the only one that merits a special name and status as an event that revolves around the cooking and eating of crawfish.

Crawfish boils are common spring social events in south Louisiana. They are usually held at homes or camps, and large numbers of relatives and friends attend. The event requires the presence of a group of people, since a forty-pound sack of live crawfish—the amount in which they are sold—yields enough for eight to ten diners, and since boiling crawfish entails a considerable amount of work. Boiling crawfish for two or three people "isn't worth the trouble," Cajuns say. Individuals who want to eat boiled crawfish in small groups go to a restaurant or buy boiled crawfish at a seafood market. A crawfish boil with ten or twelve participants is by no means a "large" crawfish boil. (The Breaux Bridge Crawfish Festival described in chapter 4, which has up to 100,000 people attending, has been dubbed "the world's largest crawfish boil.") Both hosting *and* attending a crawfish boil require a repertoire of cultural knowledge and skills likely to be possessed only by south Louisianans.

In late winter Cajuns begin to pay special attention to the size, quality, and price of the initial crawfish harvests. Crawfish become a common topic of conversation, and each week the St. Martin Parish newspaper, the *Teche News*, summarizes the latest crawfish-related data in its editorial column. As the harvest increases and the price drops, usually by March, crawfish consumption all forms greatly increases and continues through May, after which the price again rises and the quality and volume drop.

The advent of crawfish farming has expanded the availability of live crawfish beyond the old seasonal limits just described, but few Cajuns in

Above: Tourists and locals watch as a pig is killed and butchered in the traditional way at the Grand Boucherie des Cajuns in St. Martinville (Photo by Philip Gould); *left:* Fisherman empties crawfish trap in the Atchafalaya Basin, the major source of wild crawfish. Most crawfish marketed today are farmraised. (Photo by Ginette Vachon)

Machine used for sorting crawfish according to size (Photo by Barry Ancelet)

Women are usually the cooks for family meals and Sunday or holiday dinners in south Louisiana. Cooking is also a valued skill for men—especially for outdoor or large-scale events. (Photo by Ginette Vachon)

Above: Traditional Cajun snack foods such as boudin and cracklings share billing with Cajun egg rolls, a recent development in the ongoing evolution of Cajun food. (Photo by Barry Ancelet)

Above: Mardi Gras runner returns to town with chicken for communal gumbo. (Photo by Jay Elledge); *right:* Festival-goers peeling and eating crawfish at newspaper-covered table (Photo by Philip Gould)

Butchering of hog at family boucherie (Photo by Ginette Vachon)

Billboard on I-10 at Breaux Bridge for Mulate's, "The World's Most Famous Cajun Restaurant." Restaurants in Acadiana cater to tourists' and locals' interest in Cajun food and culture. (Photo by Barry Ancelet)

Men's cooking traditions are passed to younger generations of boys. Here a boy watches men clean rabbits in preparation for cooking. (Photo by Barry Ancelet)

Left: Homemade pig roaster. Innovation in cooking equipment and techniques is an ongoing process in south Louisiana. (Photo by Barry Ancelet)

Right: This specially designed crawfish table with disposal in middle makes crawfish-eating more convenient in restaurants. (Photo by Barry Ancelet)

Above: Peppers in box as lagniappe—something extra—for store patrons (Photo by Barry Ancelet)

"Cajun fire" vending machine at New York City airport—the word "Cajun" is used outside of Louisiana as a marketing term synonymous with "peppery." (Photo by Barry Ancelet)

Home vegetable garden in Lafayette. Because people prefer fresh vegetables, gardens are common sites in urban as well as rural areas of Acadiana. (Photo by Barry Ancelet)

Roadside shrimp sellers provide fresh product to inlanders. Coastal seafoods have become regional favorites associated with many Cajun dishes. (Photo by Barry Ancelet)

Crawfish in Breaux Bridge Festival parade (Photo by Philip Gould)

St. Martin Parish have crawfish boils, or eat crawfish in any form, out of season. Part of the reason for their abstinence is higher prices, but many locals also insist that farm-raised crawfish and/or frozen crawfish from any source are inferior in taste to the fresh, wild crawfish available only during the natural season. Breaux Bridge natives claim to be able to tell the difference in taste between fresh Atchafalaya crawfish and frozen or farm-raised crawfish. To crawfish aficionados, off-season crawfish are for tourists.

People usually acquire live crawfish for crawfish boils by purchasing them in forty-pound sacks. Sometimes a crawfish-catching expedition is part of the party, and some or all of the guests participate. It is necessary to have at least four pounds of live crawfish per diner, and perhaps even more. Adjustments in this estimate are based on the number of guests who are children or who are known to be heavy eaters. The people who handle the sacks, usually men, must be careful not to crush or overheat the animals, just as professional dealers must.

When the guests and the crawfish arrive at the designated location, the ensuing activities become a community project. Since boiling crawfish is a messy, odor-producing activity that takes a lot of space, most crawfish boils take place outside. The job of preparing and boiling crawfish is men's work. The host and some of the male guests remove the crawfish from the sacks, sorting out any dead ones or debris, and put the live ones in a tub of water to remove any mud and to allow the crawfish to "clean themselves out." Many locals believe that the water "purges" the crawfish. Some people add salt to the water in the belief that the salt aids in internal cleaning. The Louisiana Cooperative Extension Service recommends against this practice, saying that it puts the crawfish under stress (Moody, 1980:5).

Sorting and cleaning crawfish require dexterity to avoid being pinched by the animals' claws, and workers must take care to prevent the escape of any of the animals. Children especially enjoy this stage of the crawfish boil. They may encourage the crawfish to seize sticks with their claws, or one child may carefully pick up an animal from the rear and tease other children or other crawfish with it. These children learn how to handle crawfish through playing with them and through the intermittent lecturing they receive from the men during the process. Grandfathers and fathers pass on their expertise when they teach children, usually boys, the fine points of handling, sorting, cleaning, cooking, and evaluating crawfish.

Meanwhile, some of the other men and the women prepare and gather together at the boiling site the other necessary ingredients: salt, red (cayenne) pepper, packets of commercial "crab boil" (a seasoning mix consisting of bay leaves, thyme, cloves, marjoram, red pepper, and black pepper, used for boiling crustaceans), new potatoes, halved lemons, halved corn on the cob, halved or whole onions, and perhaps cloves of garlic and carrots. Local grocery stores sometimes shelve these items together in special displays during crawfish season. The guests drink beer or soft drinks, and when the crawfish are clean and the guests are hungry, the men prepare the cooking pot. Many Cajun families own equipment specially designed for boiling large quantities of crawfish or other crustaceans. This equipment is sold at local hardware stores, sporting goods stores, discount stores, or department stores, and in cities it can be rented. The cooking pot is a large, straight-sided, metal container with a matching metal basket that fits inside, or it may be a large metal garbage can, never used for garbage, with an improvised inner basket. Sometimes there is no inner basket, and a basket attached to a long handle is used instead. The outdoor heat source is usually a butane burner connected to a portable butane tank. The pot rests over the fire on a heavy metal tripod. Local people make or purchase tripods at stores or from handymen who make their own versions. The men use a garden hose to fill the pot with the twenty or so gallons of water required for boiling forty pounds of crawfish. (Less water is used if the crawfish are to be steam-cooked in a closed pot, as some people prefer.)

Some Cajun homes and camps have additional, more elaborate boiling facilities, such as an outdoor boiling area protected from the weather by roofing; an easily movable, suspended apparatus used to lift the heavy pot from the fire; a permanent, less troublesome heat source; copious, permanent outdoor counter space; and a built-in outdoor cooler that holds a keg of beer conveniently near the cooking site.

The host is in charge of seasoning the water, but other men oversee this process. The correct proportion of seasonings is crucial, since it is a major determinant of the taste of the finished product. Underseasoned crawfish are a particular disappointment. Red pepper, salt, lemons, and crab boil are added to the water as it is heated. Some people save the salt until later in the process (see below). The cook does not measure these ingredients according to an established recipe. Red pepper is often the predominant seasoning; about one cup (or more) is used for a forty-pound batch. The men stir, taste, and discuss the seasoned water, and they may decide to add more of one or more of the seasoning ingredients. When the seasoning is agreed upon as "right" (not always an easily reached decision) and the water is boiling, they add the vegetables to the pot. The vegetables may be removed when they are done, or they may be left in the pot throughout the cooking process. The men lower the crawfish into the pot in the metal basket, or they scoop them into the pot with a long-handled basket. When the water returns to a boil, in about ten minutes, the crawfish are boiled for about five to ten more minutes. The "correct" timing, like the "correct" seasoning, is a topic of considerable male conversation. Overcooked crawfish are mushy and difficult to peel, so the men take samples and test them for doneness by peeling and eating them. Some people place a lid on the pot during the cooking. The pros and cons of using a lid may also be a topic of debate.

Meanwhile, the people who are not directly involved in the cooking process, usually women, have prepared the tables—often long picnic tables with benches, placed end to end—by covering them with newspaper. Newspaper is the classic serving "plate" at a crawfish boil, but sometimes plastic or cardboard trays may be added as serving plates and debris collectors, especially if mosquitoes or bad weather force the meal to be eaten inside, or if the crawfish boil is an unusually formal one. Knives are sometimes available if the crawfish are large, since some people like to crack the claws for their additional small amount of meat. Sometimes bread and/or a bottled or homemade seafood dip are placed on the table. Rolls of paper towels are also available.

The crawfish are served by the men, who lift the heavy basket from the pot and pour the crawfish, mixed randomly with the vegetables, onto the tables in a great mound that extends the full length of the tables. The food fills almost the entire table space, leaving just enough room around the edges for drinks and maneuvering. If the cooking water has not been salted, it is at this point that the cook liberally pours salt over the pile of unpeeled crawfish ("that way you get just the right amount of salt on your fingers when you peel the crawfish"). There is no attempt to divide the crawfish into equal portions for each person, and there are no premarked or clearly defined "places" at the table.

Once the crawfish have been served, people sit down—in some cases, they rush to sit down—and begin to peel and eat the still-hot crawfish. Each person reaches for crawfish from the part of the pile nearest to him or her; if one part of the mound diminishes more quickly than another, the crawfish are pushed around on the table so that everyone has easy access to the food. People eat from the community serving until the supply runs out. If there are more crawfish to be boiled, the host, with less help (and advice) from the other men, who are now busy eating, begins cooking another batch, which he later pours on top of whatever remains of the first batch.

A diner peels and eats crawfish one at a time, usually in quick and steady succession. Peeling is a prerequisite to eating and involves several steps. First, the diner breaks the tail from the "head," actually the head and thorax. Then he removes the first two or three segments of the forward section of the tail shell, plus legs, from the tail meat. He holds the exposed part of the tail meat in one hand, while squeezing and pulling the rear end of the tail with his other hand. This manipulation should separate the meat in one piece from the tail shell, leaving the inedible intestinal vein in the shell rather than still attached to the meat. If the vein remains on the meat, it must be plucked off. This is usually a simple process, since the vein is loosely attached to the meat. However, the diner must be careful not to crush the vein and thus empty its contents, referred to as crawfish "shit," on the meat. The peeling technique described here may vary. Experienced Cajuns peel crawfish so quickly that it is difficult to see the exact technique they use. The description given here artificially divides a fluid process into understandable "steps." These steps are often used by Cajuns themselves to illustrate the process, in slow motion, for beginners—children and outsiders.

As the diner pops the peeled tail meat into his mouth, he reaches for another crawfish or pauses to give attention to the crawfish fat. He may extract the fat from the open end of the crawfish head with a finger, or he may place the open end of the head into his mouth, gently squeeze it, and suck the fat and other juices directly into his mouth. He may also pause to crack a large claw by hitting it with a knife handle; the small shreds of claw meat can then be picked out with the knife or a finger. If the claw has been opened skillfully, the shell can easily be removed, leaving the claw meat conveniently attached to a tough, flat, supporting structure, which is itself attached to one of the pincers. In such cases, the diner removes the meat from the supporting structure with his teeth. Intermittently, the diner stops eating crawfish in order to take a bite from a vegetable or a swallow of beer or soft drink. The crawfish and vegetables are hot with both pepper and heat, so cold liquids are consumed freely during the meal.

Usually a person peels his or her own crawfish. However, a mother may peel crawfish for her young children, teaching them the process at the same time. Children begin to eat crawfish as soon as they are old enough to eat solid foods, such as meat, but they may be six or seven years old before they can adequately peel crawfish on their own. Younger children may try to peel a few, or they may simply play with the crawfish while older guests supply them with meat. Sometimes a guest who has finished early may peel crawfish for another guest, often a spouse. The speed and dexterity with which a person peels crawfish determine the number of crawfish he or she consumes. A hearty appetite and good peeling ability are both valued, and people may call attention to the large pile of discarded shells near their places, sometimes in mock dismay and sometimes with open bragging. The diners encourage each other to eat until the crawfish are gone, and some guests acknowledge that they can barely move after the meal is over.

Conversation at a crawfish boil covers various topics, but it tends to center on the food itself, more so than at other meals. Participants compliment the chef(s) and comment on the size, flavor, and ease of peeling offered by the crawfish currently being harvested. They also discuss the volume and price of the current harvest. Discussion of these factors leads to comparisons between this batch of crawfish and previous batches earlier in the season, or to comparisons between this year's harvest and harvests of the past.

The meal ends when all the food has been consumed, or when the participants acknowledge that they are incapable of eating the entire supply. During the meal the host or hostess may occasionally gather discarded heads and shells from the table and place them in a plastic garbage bag. Those remaining on the table when the meal is over are wrapped in the newspaper as it is removed from the table. The debris is sealed in plastic garbage bags, a modern invention that has eased the problems of disposing of the remains of a crawfish boil. Crawfish shells quickly spoil and give off a strong, offensive odor. Because crawfish shells attract flies, dogs, and raccoons, it is against the law in Breaux Bridge to put them in ordinary garbage cans. However, the law is rarely enforced if the shells are tightly sealed in plastic so that no odor escapes. Even so, covered dumpsters are preferred disposal sites, but few homes have these. If a crawfish boil is held several days before scheduled garbage pickups, the ability of even the tightly sealed plastic bags to hold in the odor is questionable. Occasionally property owners are dismayed to find the remnants of someone else's crawfish boil on their vacant lots or in their garbage cans.

Participants must thoroughly wash their hands, and often their faces and forearms as well, after eating boiled crawfish. They wipe off the obvious juices with paper towels and then proceed to the garden hose for several washings with soap. Scrubbing with lemons helps eliminate the odor of crawfish from under the fingernails. If the crawfish have been served indoors, the hostess may supply the guests with bowls of lemon-scented water for preliminary washing. It is considered bad form to use a bathroom sink for initial washings. A person who does so is likely to leave crawfish juice on everything he touches, including the soap, and children are warned against so soiling the hosts' home. If a person does not wash thoroughly, his hands may smell like crawfish even the next day. If he must remove a contact lens or otherwise touch his eyes, he will quickly learn that hands that look clean may require several additional washings before all the red pepper is removed.

OTHER CRAWFISH DISHES

In all other crawfish dishes, the tail meat is prepeeled by the cook or a processing plant and combined with various other ingredients to produce the finished dish. None of these dishes is necessarily served to a large group of guests: these dishes may be served at special occasions where guests are present, or they may be served as part of an ordinary family meal. None of these dishes is associated with outdoor cooking and eating, and all are served on plates or in bowls and eaten with forks or spoons.

Women are more likely to cook these dishes, although it is not uncommon for a man to do so.

Some of the dishes made of peeled tail meat are traditional south Louisiana or Cajun dishes (see chapter 2): crawfish étouffée, gumbo, stew, jambalaya, bisque, boulettes (balls or patties), and fried crawfish tails. Of these, crawfish bisque is the only one that incorporates a nonedible portion of the animal into the finished product—cleaned crawfish heads filled with a stuffing made of ground tail meat, bread crumbs, and seasonings float in a thick broth along with whole peeled tails. (Sometimes browned stuffed heads are served alone as hors d'oeuvres.) Of all the traditional crawfish dishes, bisque is by far the most time-consuming and troublesome to prepare. For this reason, it is rarely prepared in the home today, except for very special occasions.

Peeled tail meat is also used in decidedly nontraditional dishes. Some of these follow locally perceived gourmet aesthetics: crawfish crêpes, crawfish Newburg, crawfish quiche, crawfish with Béarnaise sauce. Others are designed with cost or calories in mind, such as crawfish casseroles and crawfish salads. Tail meat is also used in dishes that in Acadiana are foreign or ethnic, such as crawfish pizza or stir-fried crawfish with Chinese vegetables and soy sauce. Some local people who are especially interested in culinary experimentation create all manner of new crawfish dishes at home. For example, one Breaux Bridge native invented the crawfish hot dog, a thick étouffée served on a bun, which is a popular item at the Crawfish Festival.

6.

The Meaning of Crawfish

How do the foodways associated with crawfish contribute to the efficacy of the crawfish as a Cajun symbol? Foodways such as the crawfish boil, described in chapter 5, underlie the use of the crawfish as a symbol, helping to determine its significance and its success. The crawfish boil, as a social event, makes a statement about both the internal unity and the boundaries of the group known as Cajuns.

GROUP UNITY AT THE CRAWFISH BOIL

The crawfish boil is an event that celebrates Cajun joie de vivre and esprit de corps. A crawfish boil, unlike most meals, demands the presence of a large group of people. Because so many relatives and friends are not ordinarily together in one place and at one time, the crawfish boil provides a welcome setting for socializing and play beyond the bounds of the nuclear family. A grandmother says that hosting a crawfish boil gives her an "excuse" to get her children and grandchildren together, a rarity now that they have scattered to several nearby towns. Another woman says, "Crawfish are as good a reason as any for a party, and better than most." At a crawfish boil, participants of all ages make play out of activities that would be considered work in an everyday context; getting, cleaning,

96

sorting, cooking, and peeling crawfish. Cajuns believe that they excel at having a good time, and a crawfish boil is the kind of event that confirms this belief.

A crawfish boil also helps validate Cajuns' belief in their environmental competence. Even though most people obtain their live crawfish from seafood markets, participants still must control the animals, which are associated with a traditional Cajun occupation that is carried out in a swampy environment. The crawfish at the cooking scene are no less ready to escape or pinch people's fingers than are those in the natural environment. The preparation and cooking of crawfish are handled by those Cajuns who are most familiar with wild animals and the natural environment—that is, men. Cooking crawfish also involves some of the skills and risks associated with the modern industrial work environment. The commonly used butane burner and tank are potential fire hazards, especially on a day when the wind makes the relatively large flame difficult to control. Men must safely lift or move heavy, hot equipment; when they do so, children are shooed away in case an accident should occur.

The sequence of events at a crawfish boil shows that the quality of a finished dish depends not only on actual cooking skills, but also on the preliminary skills of obtaining (either by trapping or by going to the best seafood market) preferred, high-quality ingredients and preparing them for cooking. At most ordinary meals in Acadiana and elsewhere in the United States, some of the preliminary steps that affect the quality of the finished dish do not take place at the scene of the meal and are not performed by any of those present. For example, the quality of a roast beef dinner depends not only on the skills of the cook, but also on the competence of the rancher who raised the steer, the slaughterhouse that did the butchering, the truckers and distributors responsible for getting the meat to the grocery store, and the retail butchers who trimmed and packaged the roast. At a crawfish boil, there is no such division of labor among a specialized, anonymous chain of workers, although commercial processing plants allow modern Cajuns to avoid some of the preliminary steps. Still, the men at a crawfish boil carry out several tasks that would ordinarily be done by anonymous workers, and they display their skills in a semipublic context.

Crawfish boils unite even the most urban Cajuns to their traditional natural environment. The crawfish is one of the few animals that normally arrive at the modern meal site alive and active. Today, most animals to be eaten are killed long before they are cooked and at sites far removed from the meal site. Crawfish, however, are killed by the cooking water; their transformation from a part of nature, an animal, to a part of culture, an edible food, takes place abruptly when they are poured into the boiling water. Until that point, the main course is very obviously a living animal: crawfish in a holding tub squirm, crawl, make hissing and bubbling sounds, and try to escape or pinch the fingers of their handlers. After being poured into the cooking pot, they briefly attempt to escape the boiling water. Even after they are thoroughly cooked, they retain their natural form. Except for their now bright red rather than muddy color and their curled-up tails, edible, cooked crawfish look exactly like living crawfish. At a crawfish boil, it is the individual diner who destroys the animal form of the food by breaking it apart and peeling it. The presence of the live or lifelike crawfish is a reminder that humans derive their sustenance from nature, from other living beings. The crawfish is also a reminder that Cajuns derive (or traditionally derived) their sustenance from the south Louisiana natural environment. It is noteworthy that live crawfish are seldom brought into a house, the sphere of human culture. Instead, the food event is moved into the yard, a part of nature that is culturally controlled. The obvious presence of "nature" at a "cultural" event is limited to this ambiguous border area, and it is here that the unusually obvious and readily perceivable transformation of an animal into food takes place.

The cooking, serving, and eating of boiled crawfish require an unusual degree of intimacy among participants and between participants and their food, as well as between humans and animals. Guests and hosts alike work together to prepare a shared meal, blurring the usual distinction between hosts as providers of food and guests as recipients. Intimacy among participants is enhanced by how the food is served. An individual is not allotted his "own" portion of crawfish; he eats from the communal pile. Nor does he have his "own" clearly marked territory of table space. Because there is one communal serving of food, everyone must be able to reach it. The use of long benches rather than individual chairs is more practical when people must crowd around a table; participants share their furniture as well as their food.

The intimacy among participants is paralleled by intimacy between participants and their food. People eat with their hands; they do not use utensils that put a physical barrier between skin and food. To participate in a crawfish boil, a person must be willing to tolerate the close presence of the living animal, and he must also be willing and able to deal with the crawfish's animal form *after* it is cooked. To peel a crawfish, a person must have an understanding of its anatomy and a willingness to see and touch its unclean, inedible parts as well as its edible parts. Sucking the head requires the diner to put the inedible, life-like head, which later becomes part of the garbage, directly into his mouth. Some Cajuns apparently find this practice a bit too intimate, as they refuse to carry out this "disgusting" act. Instead, they use a finger to extract the fat from the head.

The physical structure of the main dish itself suggests a theme of unity. Only one pot is used for cooking, and the crawfish are cooked together with the other ingredients. These ingredients are not separated and sorted for serving; there are no discrete mounds of corn or potatoes on the table. Instead, these are randomly mixed in with the crawfish in a single, large pile. The food as served is not contained by serving plates or bowls; it spills over into the spaces in front of each person, where dishes would contain food at ordinary meals. There is no clear distinction between the public mound and the private supply, as there would be if plates were used.

Crawfish foodways are shared by all Cajuns, and these foodways are flexible enough to conform to the values and styles of different types of Cajuns. There is no faction within the group for whom crawfish are inaccessible, offensive, or unknown. For example, the shared knowledge and experiences related to crawfish foodways unite the generations, and the associated skills are still passed informally from one generation to the next. Young Cajuns today often learn modern occupational skills in an institutional rather than family setting, and these skills are often different from those known and used by their more traditional parents or grandparents. However, young Cajuns today still learn from their elders how to catch (or buy), cook, and eat crawfish. There has been no tendency for crawfish-related foodways to disappear among the young. Crawfish procurement today may be a relatively traditional occupation, as in the case of independent Atchafalaya Basin fishermen, or a modern one, as in the case of crawfish farmers; it may even be a recreational pursuit, as in the case of those people who choose to spend a weekend afternoon catching crawfish for the fun of it. Young Cajuns may participate in any of these activities. In addition, virtually all Cajuns except infants and people with dietary restrictions eat crawfish. I have never met or heard of a Cajun who claims to dislike crawfish as food, or who claims that live or boiled crawfish are repellent.

A Matter of Style

Crawfish foodways can be adapted to conform to the values and styles of different groups of Cajuns. For example, crawfish may be treated as a high-status food item, acceptable to the elite class or those who aspire to it. Relatively expensive tail meat may be combined with cream, wine, mushrooms, or other costly ingredients to produce any number of refined dishes appropriate for posh dining. Expensive restaurants in Acadiana that advertise their cuisine as "gourmet" offer crawfish-stuffed avocado, crawfish Newburg, crawfish crêpes, crawfish with brandy sauce, and crawfish cocktails (boiled, peeled tail meat arranged around the rim of a bowl of dip)—dishes that would seldom grace the tables of average Cajuns. Numerous local cookbooks include recipes for such dishes. Both the restaurants and the cookbooks also identify traditional crawfish dishes, such as étouffée or bisque, as gourmet foods. Stores promote nonfood items that can be used to dress up a crawfish boil: crawfish napkins, napkin rings, place mats, trays, glasses, wine coolers, centerpieces, and even butane tanks designed with appearance in mind. A well-to-do individual could also purchase a complete set of crawfish-emblazoned (actually lobster-emblazoned) Bavarian fine china for serving all types of crawfish dishes. Cajun-style crawfish boils are especially impressive to the many Canadian and French visitors in Louisiana, who are amazed when served mounds of crawfish, an extremely expensive food item in their home countries.

A meal of crawfish is an appropriate setting for business transactions, and Lafayette restaurants offer crawfish as part of their business luncheons. Sometimes local business leaders have gone to great lengths to impress their clients with crawfish, as this news item illustrates:

> Lafayette's fame as a garden city, a mecca for gourmet food and a "can do" community of decision-makers is well-known in Abu Dhabi, United Arab Emirates.

One of Acadiana's ambassadors of good will and international trade development is Huey Lambert, vice-president of AMASAR (American Associates of Arabia), and he provides this latest report. The Mansoori Oil field Division held its second annual "Louisiana Crawfish Dinner Beach Party" in Abu Dhabi on May 24 [1979]. It was a huge success.

Huey brought 120 pounds of crawfish for the party; next year he'll have to increase the figure to 300 pounds. Around 200 people attended, 50 from Louisiana, others from France and the Middle East. They loved the food seasoned with south Louisiana pepper sauce.

Huey met a Texan in London who offered $500 for one of the two containers of live Louisiana crawfish. The AMASAR exec turned him down (B. Angers 1979:13)

Organizers of conventions held in south Louisiana can hire local caterers who will provide a complete crawfish boil party—starting with live crawfish—for conventioneers.

Even though the crawfish is a high-status food in many contexts today, Cajuns are aware of the food's former low status and of the fact that some outsiders today still see crawfish as repulsive (see below). Some Cajuns draw on this awareness and playfully emphasize those aspects of crawfish foodways that are most compatible with an informal, earthy style. For example, a crawfish boil can provide an occasion for very heavy eating, drinking, and "partying," for those who are so inclined. The difficult work required at a crawfish boil provides an opportunity for showing off physical strength and skill. Moreover, some Cajuns emphasize the *least* refined aspects of eating crawfish. For example in the early 1980s a local tee shirt bore the words "I suck heads," a statement that reflected the then high-profile "Coonass" style in its obscene connotations and its flaunting of a practice that is found to be especially repulsive by some outsiders and by some Cajuns as well. Another tee shirt of the same period was illustrated with a picture of a crawfish, accompanied by the slogan "Eat my tail." The following joke combines the imagery of both tee-shirt slogans:

Q: Why do crawfish like Coonasses [or Cajuns]?
A: Because Coonasses [or Cajuns] are the only people who are willing to suck their heads and eat their tails.

CRAWFISH EATING AND ETHNIC BOUNDARIES

Although Cajuns have appropriated the crawfish as their ethnic symbol, they are not the only people in south Louisiana who catch, cook, and eat crawfish. Since most other long-time residents do likewise, crawfish food-ways do not distinguish Cajuns from non-Cajun south Louisianans. Rather, knowledge of crawfish foodways distinguishes Cajuns (and, pre-sumably, other south Louisianans) from newcomers or outsiders, most of whom are English-speaking "Americans." Outsiders are marked as dif-ferent by their initial inability to peel and eat boiled crawfish or by their refusal to recognize crawfish as food.

Because of the large numbers of newcomers in Acadiana today, it is not unusual for a non-Cajun coworker, friend, or relative to be invited to a crawfish boil or to order boiled crawfish in a restaurant. Novices who are served their first pile of boiled crawfish find themselves in the unusual position of not knowing how to eat the food as served. Cajuns joke about outsiders who try to eat the head of the crawfish, or who eat the inedible intestinal vein by mistake, or who tear up the meat in removing it from the shell, or who take a full five minutes to peel and eat a single crawfish, or who ask their hosts or waitresses for forks, or who cannot tolerate the high pepper content of the crawfish, or who absentmindedly rub an eye with a pepper-covered finger, or who are foolish enough to wear their best clothes to a crawfish boil. In order to eat properly (or to eat at all) a novice must receive help from insiders—from dining companions or, if in a restaurant setting, from a waitress or friendly customers at a nearby table. In such situations, the social significance of being Cajun and of being non-Cajun is intensified. Cajuns hold the knowledge and skills that are the key to the situation, and they play the role of teachers or parents in relation to the outsiders. The outsiders, like children, must be taught how to do something as simple and basic as eating. In contrast to Cajuns, the outsiders play the role of ignorant, inept beginners—a position similar to that of very young Cajun children. The relative status of these roles is the reverse of what prevailed during the initial days of modernization and Americanization in Acadiana, when Cajuns were often the people who lacked the situationally relevant knowledge and skills. Cajuns seem to enjoy, in a nonmalicious way, the awkwardness of outsiders and the oppor-tunity to teach others to eat and enjoy crawfish. One local person com-ments, "Why do you think Cajuns always try to serve boiled crawfish to outsiders? We like to watch them try to peel crawfish. It's funny. Cajuns can giggle and say, 'You like that, eh?'" Such opportunities may be particularly satisfying for those Cajuns who have experienced the prejudice of outsiders in situations in which Cajuns have been the novices.

Although the food-related skills necessary for eating boiled crawfish distinguish insiders from outsiders and thus highlight ethnic boundaries, the food events at which boiled crawfish are served are themselves settings for friendly socializing among all participants, regardless of ethnicity. Crawfish food events do not entail the social exclusion of outsiders; rather, they provide opportunities for *including* outsiders in the local social sphere. The social distinction between Cajuns and outsiders is relevant only when the outsiders are being taught the necessary skills; after they have successfully completed their initiation and are capable of peeling and eating crawfish using Cajun know-how, the social distinctions become irrelevant. Thus, even though an event such as a crawfish boil reinforces Cajun social identity, it is at the same time an appropriate setting for socializing between insiders and outsiders. A newcomer at a crawfish boil shares the "intimacy" of the event as described earlier. Cajuns are pleased when newcomers are successful in learning to eat crawfish, and they point with pride to the many "Americans" in Acadiana who have become avid crawfish eaters. A newcomer's conversion to crawfish foodways validates Cajuns' perception of their lifestyle as especially appealing to outsiders (see the introduction). It also is a reminder of the traditional Cajun ability to absorb and acculturate others—an ability that has been less effective in the larger social sphere since the acceleration of the Americanization and modernization of the twentieth century.

Visitors and tourists who come to Acadiana seldom have the opportunity to attend a Cajun family crawfish boil, but they do have the opportunity to eat crawfish in one of several forms in the many tourist-oriented Cajun restaurants in the region. As is the case with other ethnically marked tourist attractions, such restaurants are more than a boon to the local economy. Like home crawfish boils, the restaurants provide an environment in which outsiders are the novices and insiders are the teachers. The fact that tourists flock to these restaurants is flattering as well as lucrative for Cajuns. The same is true of the Breaux Bridge Crawfish Festival (see chapter 4).

Not all outsiders, however, are willing or successful crawfish-eating converts. Several newcomers in Acadiana have told me that their first crawfish boil was their last. These people enjoy peeled tail meat as part of elaborate dishes, but they avoid boiled crawfish and crawfish boils. I once observed a native of the western United States at his first and last crawfish boil. He struggled to peel and eat three crawfish and then stopped eating, claiming that he was no longer hungry. He also complained that the shells were cutting his fingers and that the pepper was irritating the cuts. His failure to enjoy a meal that had been presented with pride and aplomb was obviously embarrassing to both him and his hosts. A native of New York says that her only crawfish boil was "interesting, but not interesting enough to make a habit of it." Her account suggests that a meal of boiled crawfish violates her definition of a proper meal:

> When I arrived at the house, I wondered why the table wasn't set. When people invite guests for dinner, they usually go out of their way to make the tables nice. When they started putting newspaper on the table, I thought it was a joke. I couldn't believe it when they poured the crawfish on the newspaper—nothing but tiny lobsters, piles of tiny lobsters, and a few potatoes—not even a salad. The crawfish were good, but they're not worth the trouble. I'll admit that when I go out to dinner, it's a special occasion, and I don't want to have to get my hands dirty. I love crawfish étouffée, and I like the taste of boiled crawfish, but I don't want to peel them.

Some outsiders refuse to eat boiled crawfish because they are bothered by the presence of the living animal at the meal site shortly before the meal is served, or because they are disturbed by the lifelike appearance of the boiled crawfish. One newcomer explains that while he enjoys crawfish dishes that contain tail meat, the sight of the living animal he is going to eat at a crawfish boil causes him to lose his appetite. He admits that his reaction is illogical, saying, "I know that for every hamburger I eat, someone killed a cow. But the difference is, I didn't have to watch." Another man, a native of north Texas, recalls his only encounter with boiled crawfish in these words: "A Cajun I work with had been trying to get me to eat boiled crawfish ever since I moved here. I managed to avoid the issue for quite a while. Then one night he tricked me. He invited me over for a beer, and when I got there he brought out a paper bag of leftover boiled crawfish. He poured some on a plate and put it in front of me. I looked down, and all I could see was eyes staring back at me, dozens of little black eyes. And antennas. And legs." This man's story brings up a problem that is not uncommon among outsiders who are offered boiled crawfish: not only does the food look like a living animal but, more specifically, it looks like a particular type of living animal—an insect. Boiled crawfish retain their small, segmented bodies, hard shells, multiple legs, antennas, and protruding eyes. Indeed, crawfish are often called mudbugs. Since few people in the United States eat insects—indeed, most Americans find the thought revolting—it is not uncommon for outsiders to avoid eating what they perceive as an insectlike creature. These same people may willingly eat prepared tail meat, which resembles peeled shrimp (more likely a familiar and high-status food to most outsiders) and does not conjure up images of insects in one's plate.

Some outsiders refuse to eat crawfish in any form. They classify crawfish as fish bait—not human food—or as vermin, partly because of the creature's insectlike appearance and partly because of its natural habitat. They believe that crawfish are unsanitary animals because they live in muddy areas at the bottom of streams and ditches. Recreational crawfishermen are often seen along roadside ditches bordering local highways. These drainage ditches are accessible, fertile sources of crawfish, but some outsiders are particularly biased against eating food they believe comes from a roadside ditch. (Of course, commercial crawfish do not come from roadside ditches.) Cajuns are likely to be insulted by such sentiments, which imply that Cajuns eat filth. In my observation, confirmed crawfish avoiders who classify crawfish as vermin are relatively rare today, or at least they do not advertise their beliefs as they reportedly did in the past. However, they are apparently still numerous enough to remind Cajuns that their favorite food (and their chosen emblem) has sometimes been an object of outsiders' scorn.

People who cannot or will not eat crawfish may be laughed at, pitied, or resented, and they are not likely to be invited to a meal at which crawfish are served. However, such people are not avoided by Cajuns in other social settings solely because they do not eat crawfish. Some Cajuns are married to people who do not eat crawfish and/or who view the crawfish as repulsive and inedible. I once observed such a couple eating in a local seafood restaurant with their two-year-old child. The husband, a Cajun, ordered a platter of boiled crawfish; the wife, an Anglo southerner, ordered fried shrimp. When the food arrived, the wife instructed her husband to keep his tray of crawfish well to his side of the table. The husband gave the little boy a crawfish to play with and several pieces of peeled tail meat. The wife expressed disgust and squeamishness each time the child reached for the unpeeled crawfish, telling him not to touch it and that it was dirty. Each time the child hesitated at his mother's urging, the father pushed the crawfish toward him. This battle over the child's future food habits—and, by implication, the battle over his future ethnic identity—ended without a clear victory for either side.

THE CRAWFISH AS ANIMAL AND SYMBOL

So far, I have referred to the crawfish as animal only in situations in which the animal is also an incipient food. However, the crawfish may also be viewed as an animal that exists in the local environment, independent of its role as food. In this sense the crawfish is used as a symbol that communicates additional meaning, which cannot be derived from analyzing its role as food. The dual role of the crawfish as food and as animal in Cajun life is partly responsible for the crawfish's success as an ethnic symbol.

Crawfish and Cajuns live together in the south Louisiana environment. This camaraderie is made explicit in a local "legend"—printed on souvenirs and restaurant menus—which claims that the lobsters that accompanied the Acadian refugees in their journey from Canada to Louisiana shrank into crawfish during the exhausting journey. These crawfish remained loyal friends to the Louisiana Cajuns, even modeling their chimneyed mud burrows—which today are common on the lawns of new subdivisions—after the mud chimneys on traditional Cajun houses (see, for example, L. Guirard [1973]). It is noteworthy that this popular "myth" explains the origins of Louisiana crawfish by linking the animal's ancestral origins with those of the Cajuns: both came from Canada, both survived an arduous journey, and both found haven in Louisiana.

In the legend, both the Cajuns and the crawfish are survivors in the face of hardship. The behavior of real rather than legendary crawfish suggests to humans that the crawfish is indeed a survivor, which makes the animal an especially appropriate ethnic emblem for Cajuns. Crawfish are pugnacious: they fight with each other, and they threaten their human captors with sharp claws. They are tenacious: they remain alive and active outside their natural environment longer than do most other primarily aquatic animals, and they struggle to survive even after they enter the cooking pot. They are also courageous in Cajun eyes: when threatened, they do not flee, but rather face their adversary with claws outstretched. A local joke describes a crawfish sitting on the railroad tracks, aggressively snapping its claws at an oncoming locomotive. The folksong quoted in chapter 4 says that "crawfish ain't skeered of a six-mule team." Even Cajuns, the people who believe themselves to be especially adept at handling crawfish, view the crawfish's feistiness with respect as well as humor. One writer suggests that "Cajuns have taken the animal's courage as a symbol for their own cultural revival" (Hallowell 1979:114). Although it would be more precise to say that the animal's courage is one of several factors that make the crawfish an appropriate Cajun symbol, the fighting spirit of the crawfish nevertheless contributes to the effectiveness of the symbol. The intrepidity and persistence of the crawfish are paralleled in the Cajuns' own image of themselves as environmentally competent—as people who can survive in difficult situations.

Many of the symbolic representations of the crawfish in Acadiana project upon the crawfish a generally human and specifically Cajun identity. The crawfish is presented as having human traits, such as courage and loyalty. In jokes, crawfish speak with a Cajun accent. Crawfish are frequently illustrated in humanlike form: a tee shirt bears a picture of a traditional Cajun band composed of crawfish musicians, and a decal for a local radio station shows a grinning crawfish wearing a cowboy hat, relaxing near an offshore oil rig. Several locally published children's books feature cartoonlike crawfish characters. In a book promoted by CODOFIL, crawfish are among the bilingual animals that dance at a fais do-do (Perales 1982). In some instances, it is humans who take on the characteristics of crawfish. Local people remark jokingly, after eating large quantities of crawfish, "I'll be walking backwards for a week" or "I'll be acting funny in the bathtub tonight." A very popular series of children's books, including *The Adventures of Crawfish-Man* (Edler 1979) and *Crawfish-Man Rescues Ron Guidry* (Edler 1980), feature a part-human and part-crawfish "superhéreaux" (superhero) whose goal is to "keep the peace, justice, and the Cajun way" (Edler 1979). A simple Cajun fisherman under ordinary circumstances, this comic-book-style character can transform himself into a giant, manlike crawfish who saves Cajuns in trouble and teaches Cajun children regional geography and French phrases in the process.

The personified crawfish, as a symbol, is capable of communicating a broad range of messages about being Cajun. When the crawfish is treated as a human, it can "do" and "say" anything a human can. A personified crawfish can speak French, or not speak French. It can be a native of Acadia, or it can work offshore. It can support a national political candidate, play the accordion or exhibit the ultimate degree of environmental competence (Crawfish-Man). The emblematic crawfish can make obscene suggestions in the extreme Coonass style, or it can be a well-mannered, primly dressed dancer at an old-fashioned fais do-do. Like the crawfish as food, the emblematic crawfish as animal is manipulated for various purposes by various types of Cajuns. Because the personified animal itself is made to manipulate other symbols (words, dress, facial expressions, etc.) and made to "act" in ways that are culturally significant to humans (by participating in a given occupation, recreational activity, etc.), it can be used to send messages that are much more explicit than those inherent in crawfish foodways. The personified emblematic crawfish stands for Cajuns and, like Cajuns, it enlists speech and other symbol systems to make statements about Cajun ethnicity and other matters. The emblematic crawfish also stands for crawfish, both as food and as an animal. As such, the symbolic crawfish carries all the connotations associated with the crawfish as food and as animal and thus contains subtle messages about relationships between insiders and outsiders, relationships among insiders, and interaction between humans and the natural world.

The relationship between the crawfish as symbol and Cajuns as referent is both metonymic and metaphoric. Metonymy suggests contiguity, an intrinsic relationship between the symbol and its referent (Leach 1970:47–48, 1976:14–15). The crawfish has been an intrinsic part of both traditional and modern Cajun life as a local animal, as an object of economic value, and as a food. People and crawfish share the same environment and come into physical contact (Cajuns handle crawfish). Ingestion is perhaps the ultimate form of contiguity: when a person eats food, that food becomes an intrinsic part of that person's physical self. In addition, the crawfish as food is part of a larger category of Cajun food, and as such it metonymically stands for Cajun food, which in turn is associated with Cajuns.

A metaphor asserts similarity (Leach 1970:47, 1976:14–15). The personified crawfish that stands for Cajuns is perceived as being "like"

Cajuns. As is the case with metaphor, the assertion is somewhat arbitrary. For example, the animal's defense behavior on land (slowly backing up with claws raised) is equated with (human) courage in Louisiana. However, this behavior is interpreted differently elsewhere; for example, national sportscasters use the verb *to crawfish* to describe the behavior of a boxer who lacks aggressive behavior, who timidly guards himself with his gloves while steadily backing away from his opponent. Modern media and mass marketing in Louisiana extend the crawfish/Cajun metaphor, asserting seemingly endless (and sometimes superficial or forced) similarities between crawfish and Cajuns, using additional methods of communication, such as words and dress, to drive home the message of similarity.

There is one area of similarity between Cajuns and crawfish that has not been pointed out by the regional media and that, to my knowledge, is not consciously articulated by Cajuns. This point of resemblance is that Cajuns and crawfish are both anomalies within certain contexts. Cajuns do not conform to the popular image of what Americans are like, of what southerners are like, or of what French people are like. They are little known outside their region, and the superficial attention given to them on a national level, especially through the media, often paints a distorted picture—one that is unrealistically positive or unfairly negative. Similarly, the crawfish is not easily categorized relative to many other animals, by either Cajuns or outsiders. It is a crustacean that lives in fresh water, an aquatic animal that walks on land. As a food, it is little known in the United States outside of south Louisiana, and outsiders who are familiar with crawfish tend to take extreme views toward it, seeing it either as gourmet food or repulsive vermin. Certain crawfish foodways are unusual even within the Cajun food system, especially those associated with the cooking and eating of boiled crawfish. It is appropriate that a people who see themselves as distinctive and atypical should take as a symbol an animal and a food that they and others also see as distinctive and atypical.

7.

Boucheries, Mardi Gras, and Community Festivals

The crawfish boil is a well known Cajun food-related event, and it is regarded as characteristically "Cajun" by Cajuns themselves, by the regional media, and by Anglo-American outsiders. However, Cajuns hold a variety of other social events that revolve around food and eating, and that are often regarded by Cajuns and others as characteristically "Cajun." An analysis of these events, like the analysis of crawfish boils presented in chapter 6, yields insight into the relationship between Cajun foodways and ethnic identity.

THE FAMILY BOUCHERIE

A family boucherie—not to be confused with the traditional meat-butchering and distribution institution also known as a boucherie—is an all-day, outdoor food event held during the cooler months in rural areas of Acadiana. The host is a full-time or part-time farmer, and the many guests include relatives and friends. With the help of some of the other men, the host slaughters one of his hogs, cleans it by scalding and scraping off the hair, and cuts it into usable parts, discarding those few parts which are considered inedible. Some of the men make cracklings and lard from the best cuts of fat; the cracklings, seasoned with salt and red pepper, are eaten as a snack by the participants. Other participants—traditionally the women—carry out the long and involved task of making boudin, which includes cooking the bony muscle meat; separating the bits of bone from the meat; grinding the meat and the seasoning ingredients; cooking the ground meat, ground seasonings, and organ meat together; mixing these with cooked rice; and stuffing the product into cleaned sausage casings. Participants also make other pork dishes, such as backbone stew, hogshead cheese, chaudin, and rice dressing, and they either make on location or bring from home various other dishes, such as potato salad, cooked vegetables, and desserts.

At the old, round-robin boucheries in the past, all of the highly perishable pork had to be eaten, preserved, or distributed to participants for quick use; at family boucheries today, however, whatever is not eaten immediately is relegated to the refrigerator or freezer for storage. Refrigeration has made it possible for individual families to hold fun-filled, play-oriented boucheries, independently of the older, work-oriented, round-robin system. Although today's family boucheries certainly involve work—and they fill the family freezer with meat—there is ample time at a family boucherie for play. Participants talk, relax, play games, drink, and have a leisurely, copious meal. Some hosts further reduce the workload at family boucheries, and increase the time available for play, by saving some of the more arduous tasks for later. For example, the bony parts of the hog may be frozen, and the boudin made another day.

THE COCHON DE LAIT

The French term *cochon de lait* literally means "suckling pig," and it once referred primarily to a special springtime dish, often served on Easter Sunday: roast suckling pig. Today the term *cochon de lait* is more commonly used to refer to a specific food event, that is, a hog roast. Adult hogs, rather than suckling pigs, provide the meat. A host need not be a farmer or even a rural resident to hold a cochon de lait, although he does need a yard with enough space for the required activities. The host buys a cleaned whole hog (muscle meat only) from a local slaughterhouse; with the help of some of the male guests, he roasts it with the use of some version of the hog-roasting equipment described in chapter 3. Women prepare or bring from their homes the various side dishes commonly found at family boucheries or Sunday or holiday dinners: potato salad, baked sweet potatoes, rice dressing, green peas or green beans, bread, and desserts. The guests, specially the men, watch the hog-roasting process. When the hog is cooked, everyone sits down to a full meal.

A cochon de lait does not require as much time as a family boucherie, since the lengthy butchering process is not part of the event. The event often begins during the afternoon, and the festivities may continue late into the evening. As at a family boucherie, numerous guests are invited, and various play activities take place.

RURAL MARDI GRAS

Only the oldest generation in Breaux Bridge vaguely remembers a time when local people "ran Mardi Gras" in the traditional style in that town. The rural south Louisiana custom of "running Mardi Gras" on Shrove Tuesday, the eve of Lent with its forty days of partial fasting and abstinence from meat, was abandoned by most Acadiana communities during the early twentieth century, often because of unwelcome violence associated with the event (Ancelet, Edwards, and Pitre 1991:91). During the early 1950s, the town of Mamou in Evangeline Parish revived the traditional Cajun style of Mardi Gras running, with careful attention to "authenticity" and orderly behavior. At least a dozen other Cajun towns have since followed suit. Cajuns from Breaux Bridge and elsewhere in Acadiana are familiar with traditional Mardi Gras running, even though their communities have not revived this custom. The revived Mardi Gras celebrations receive considerable regional and national media attention, and Cajuns from towns like Breaux Bridge sometimes attend the Mardi Gras festivities in Mamou and elsewhere as visitors. Thus knowledge of the event described here is not limited to those citizens whose towns have revived the old custom.

Early on Mardi Gras morning, the masked and costumed runners (always men, with some recent exceptions) leave town in an orderly group on horseback. They go from house to house in the countryside, soliciting contributions for the gumbo that is to be served at the dance that night, and issuing invitations to the dance. The maskers entertain the householders with traditional Cajun music, dancing, and festive antics, and the householders in return offer ingredients for the gumbo and perhaps a drink or snack for the runners. The preferred ingredient is a live chicken, which is often thrown into the air. The maskers chase it, catch it, wring its neck, and eventually take it to the site in town where the gumbo is to be cooked. Some householders donate rice, sausage, seasoning vegetables, or money, and some throw a packaged, frozen chicken. The riders continue their rounds for much of the day and, despite their sometimes heavy beer consumption during the run, they manage to ride back into town at the end of the day in an orderly procession, with much aplomb. Other townspeople, traditionally the women, clean the chickens and prepare the gumbo at a community kitchen or cooking site. Community members eat the gumbo and dance to Cajun music until midnight, the beginning of Lent.

Mardi Gras is unusual in that women are solely responsible for cooking the main dish for a large-scale, festive food event. As noted in earlier chapters, it is usually Cajun men who do the cooking for such events, and it is difficult for the older men who remain in town during the run to stay away from the cooking site.

COMMUNITY FESTIVALS

Commercial community festivals, such as the Breaux Bridge Crawfish Festival described in chapter 4, offer many food-related events and activities, which vary from one festival to the next. At all festivals, tourists and local people purchase prepared food, often made by locals, at various booths and temporary eateries on the fairgrounds. But it is the special, scheduled food events and related activities that receive the focused attention of festival audiences, and these are also of most interest here. These events are held at designated times and locations during the festival weekend, and they are advertised as part of the festival's "attractions."

One such event is the eating contest. A limited number of registered contestants vie to eat the most food within a specified time limit. The food is usually a local specialty, and often the one that gives the festival its name, such as boiled crawfish, rice dressing, gumbo, raw oysters, or boudin. The contestants are usually local men, although a token woman or visiting dignitary may be persuaded to enter the contest. The contest takes place in front of a large, cheering audience of tourists, locals, photographers, and television news crews, and it is overseen by judges, who make sure that the food is carefully measured or weighed and actually consumed by the contestants. The time limit is generous, so that the key factor in winning is the ability to eat a large amount of food, rather than the ability to eat quickly. The winners of the crawfish-eating contests in Breaux Bridge have each eaten, on the average, twenty-eight pounds of boiled crawfish—six to seven times the amount one would eat at a crawfish boil.

Cooking contests and demonstrations are held at many commercial festivals. Sometimes these are one and the same: contestants demonstrate their cooking skills at the fairground, and judges decide whose product is the best. In other cases, contestants cook at home and take the dish to the contest site for the taste test. Often, there are cooking demonstrations that are not part of a contest. Local cooks, often men, make large batches of jambalaya, gumbo, or boudin, both to entertain the onlookers and to sell to customers. The fact that the food is cooked in extremely large amounts is part of the attraction and novelty of these demonstrations. (As noted earlier, Cajun men tend to cook in much larger quantities than women do, because they usually cook for large outdoor social gatherings.) The Bridge City Gumbo Festival features a cast-iron gumbo pot that is five feet in diameter and three feet deep, permanently mounted on a wheeled platform base. Men stir the gumbo with "spoons" the size of shovels. Less extreme but more common festival pots are two to three feet in diameter and depth.

Contests and demonstrations of food-related skills are presented at some festivals. The contestants or demonstrators are usually local people who make their livings through these skills. For example, women who peel crawfish professionally participate in the crawfish-peeling contest at the Crawfish Festival. Men skin catfish at the Des Allemands Catfish Festival; men and women skin small game animals at the Cameron Fish and Wildlife Festival; and men chase pigs at the Basile Swine Festival, open oysters at the Galliano Oyster Festival, and carve and display duck decoys at the Lagniappe on the Bayou Festival in Chauvin. At the Grand Boucherie des Cajuns, a St. Martinville festival founded specifically for the purpose of "showing the traditional Cajun lifestyle" to younger Cajuns and outsiders, the spectators watch as a hog is slaughtered and transformed into boudin, cracklings, hogshead cheese, pork stew, and soap—all in accordance with the traditional methods of making these products.

OTHER FOOD EVENTS

In addition to crawfish boils and the other food events that have been described, there are other festive food events that are associated with being Cajun and that sometimes receive special names. For example, if a family invites a large number of people for a meal of sauce picquante, the event is called a sauce picquante. The main dish is usually cooked by men, and the event usually takes place outdoors. Other similar events include crab boils, shrimp boils, fish fries, oyster openings, and barbecues. (Any meat or fish may be grilled or smoked at a barbecue.) Gumbo or jambalaya may similarly be cooked outdoors and served to large numbers of guests; however, these events are not referred to as gumbos or jambalayas. The events listed here *may* include many guests, but they sometimes include only a few. It is easier to control the size of a pot of gumbo—and the number of guests it feeds—than it is to control the size of a whole hog, a purchased sack of live crawfish, or the amount of food one acquires during an unusually successful hunting or fishing expedition.

INTERPRETING FOOD EVENTS

Like the crawfish boil, the food events described here help express and validate Cajun environmental competence. At all these events, activities that demonstrate know-how are displayed to the participants who will share the meal. With the exception of Mardi Gras chicken chasing, these activities take place at or very near the meal site. At a family boucherie the host—who probably raised the pig himself—and his helpers demonstrate the skills and knowledge necessary for transforming an animal into usable cuts of meat. The participants then transform the meat into edible dishes. Mardi Gras runners procure food for the entire community, through a public and highly ritualized process that takes place only once a year. They demonstrate their horsemanship in a serious manner when they ride in an orderly procession in and out of town, and show it off in an exaggerated, mocking manner when they ride while facing backwards or standing up during the run itself. Although chickens are not game animals, the runners' foray into the countryside for food resembles a hunt, and their chasing of chickens resembles a predator's running down of its prey. Each runner hopes to catch at least one chicken, and a runner who catches many chickens earns special status in the eyes of his peers. Barry Ancelet, an experienced Cajun Mardi Gras runner and a folklorist who has been active in the Cajun ethnic pride movement, describes the significance of the runners' march back into town at the end of the day: "When the runners ride back into town, they're very proud of themselves. They feel like heroes returning from the hunt with food. They have a haughty attitude toward the men who spent the day in town. The runners have accomplished something, and the people who stayed in town, by comparison, are milk toast" (Ancelet 1983).

At the other food-related events as well, skills useful in the local natural environment are usually on display, publicly or semipublicly. For example, a man who is opening oysters—whether he is doing so as part of a festival contest, a festival demonstration, or his own oyster-opening party—must be able to open the tightly closed bivalve shells quickly, without tearing the oyster meat. If the host has harvested the oysters himself, then the event is an occasion that also reveals his food procurement skills. At many of the events discussed here, skills learned in the Louisiana rural-industrial setting are also evident. The presence of homemade barbecue grills, hog-roasting equipment, "Cajun microwaves," and home-built outdoor kitchens reveals a man's skill in fashioning these devices; his ability to use them effectively confirms his competence. This equipment receives considerable attention from male guests at these events.

Live animals are always present at several types of Cajun food events in addition to the crawfish boil; these include family boucheries, Mardi Gras, crab boils, and oyster openings. At all of these except Mardi Gras, the live animal is present at or near the meal site. Live animals are sometimes present at festivals, such as the Grand Boucherie des Cajuns in St. Martinville, the Crawfish Festival, the Swine Festival in Basile, and the Frog Festival in Rayne. Participants often witness the killing of the animal they will eat. The death is apparent even in the case of the immobile oysters. Oyster openers, struggling to disengage the muscle that holds the shell closed, may say, "This one doesn't want to give up" or "This is a tough one; he doesn't want to die." (An oyster that falls open easily is dead and unfit for eating.) At a cochon de lait, the pig is not alive, but it does arrive in one large piece that suggests the form of the living animal. Pictures of live animals are usually present at commercial festivals. The presence or suggested presence of live animals and the killing of live animals at these food events—as at a crawfish boil—is a reminder that humans derive their sustenance from nature, and more specifically that Cajuns derive these foods, through the use of their skills, from their south Louisiana environment.

As is the case at a crawfish boil, it is the men—those Cajuns who are most familiar with the natural environment and its associated skills—who cook. The cooking takes place outdoors, or in a man's kitchen that may also be called an outdoor kitchen, even if it is enclosed. These events, like the crawfish boil, are relegated to an ambiguous border area between nature and culture (the yard), or to an enclosed kitchen that is described *as if it were* outdoors. Moreover, all of these events except Mardi Gras and community festival activities are also commonly held at family camps—homes that are located in natural settings. Many of these events are scheduled according to natural seasons. For example, shrimp and crab boils are likely to be held in the summer when these foods are plentiful, while a boucherie or cochon de lait is likely to be held in the winter, when pigs are fat, there are fewer flies, and the outdoor temperature is cool enough for the comfort of the cooks. Many commercial festivals are held during the harvest season of the product that is the focus of the festival.

In addition to demonstrating Cajun environmental skills, the food events described here also validate Cajun sociability. These occasions show Cajuns and any outsiders who may be present that Cajuns do indeed enjoy solidarity and know how to have a good time, especially in a family- or community-oriented setting.

An everyday family meal is a social occasion that is expected to provide pleasant social interaction and culinary satisfaction. However, the food events analyzed here are special, intensified, and expanded social occasions, which center on the consumption of particularly popular types of traditional Cajun foods. These events usually involve large numbers of guests, including members of the immediate family, relatives, neighbors, close friends, new or distant friends, and, in the case of the better known Mardi Gras celebrations and commercial festivals—tourists, who are complete strangers. These events are planned in advance, and some guests come from distant locations in order to be with their friends and relatives. A boucherie, cochon de lait, or crawfish boil sometimes serves as the focus of a full-scale family reunion, and a visit from an expatriate relative or friend provides an "excuse" for holding any of these events (except

Mardi Gras or commercial festivals). Each of these events lasts longer than an ordinary meal, and guests arrive well before the food is served and stay long after it has been eaten.

The cooperation in the preparation of food at many of these events demonstrates Cajun solidarity and esprit de corps. It is not unusual for guests to contribute side dishes at a boucherie or cochon de lait, or to bring beer, or to donate money to help pay for a sack of crawfish. The participants in a boucherie work hard for hours at various tasks, and guests at most events help the host and hostess in some way. Unless they are newcomers to Acadiana who do not understand the work at hand, they rarely sit back and wait for the food to be served. Although there are many "guests" at commercial festivals who are primarily spectators (that is, tourists), the community members who host the festivals must cooperate and contribute their time and labor. Some of the larger festivals, including the Breaux Bridge Crawfish Festival, have turned over part of the enormous task of food preparation to professional food services, although some community members do continue to cook and sell food at these large festivals. For the very popular Lagniappe on the Bayou Festival in the small town of Chauvin in Terrebonne Parish, which attracts almost as many people as the Crawfish Festival, the townspeople accomplish the remarkable task of procuring and preparing by themselves virtually all the festival food. The local shrimpers donate their time and fuel to catch the shrimp, crabs, and other seafoods sold at the festival, and the townspeople work for weeks to prepare ahead those foods which can be frozen and reheated at the festival. Many of the food booths at this festival are run by families, who donate their time and their ingredients. The traditional Cajun Mardi Gras perhaps most clearly demonstrates community solidarity through food preparation and eating. Each householder contributes an ingredient to the gumbo, and each does so in a public, ritualized way—during the visit to the house by the runners. The community serves as its own "host" for the evening meal of gumbo.

A festive or playful atmosphere prevails at these food events. People do have a good time when they come together for the shared meal and its associated activities. Work itself becomes play. Butchering a hog in an everyday context is work, but butchering a hog at a family boucherie, in a festive social context, is both work and play. Mardi Gras perhaps best shows the merging of work and play. Participants go to considerable trouble to procure and prepare the ingredients for a *very* large gumbo, and they do so with a great deal of playfulness, on one of the most festive days of the year. Festival eating contests turn the act of eating into play. Although we may suspect that some individual contestants take these contests seriously—and view their ability to consume unusually large amounts of food as an admirable skill or talent, as do some onlookers—in general the tone of the event is comic and playful, as evidenced by the jokes, laughter, and smiles of the participants, judges, and onlookers.

Thus special Cajun food events demonstrate *both* environmental competence and sociability at the same time. These two aspects of Cajun identity, when exaggerated or taken out of their larger cultural context, give rise to two prevalent negative stereotypes of Cajuns. An exaggerated emphasis on environmental skills leads to the image of the isolated, xenophobic, violent swamp dweller, who is more at home in the wilds than in the company of other people. An exaggerated emphasis on sociability yields the image of the happy-go-lucky, hedonistic, lazy Cajun, who has no desire or need to work hard in such a fertile homeland. However, a Cajun or outsider who attends one of the special Cajun food events described here sees that Cajuns work hard *and* play hard. In everyday life, work and play are often relegated to separate spheres. However, food events belong to both spheres, and food itself is the product of a series of work activities that culminates in a pleasurable social activity, a good meal.

We might speculate that all food events are potential occasions for displaying and validating *both* Cajun environmental know-how and sociability. However, activities that display environmental skills are not clearly visible at most everyday domestic meals in contemporary Acadiana, and ordinary domestic meals are not called Cajun events. A family is likely to obtain the ingredients of an ordinary meal by shopping at a local grocery store, or by removing from the freezer the products of a now long-past hunting expedition, fishing trip, boucherie, or harvest. The preliminary processes that begin to transform a part of nature (plants and animals) into a part of culture (cooked dishes) have already been carried out, often by anonymous workers at a distant time or place. Animals have already been killed, dirt and debris have been discarded, certain inedible portions of some foods have been removed (hair, viscera, scales, shells, stems, husks), and large animals have been cut up into parts small enough to cook on a family stove. The preparation of an ordinary family meal does not attract the attention of an audience, and the cook often performs this task while in the midst of other activities, such as caring for children or watching television.

Activities that display sociability are ideally present to some degree at a family meal. Family members normally eat together (though conflicting daily schedules sometimes make this difficult or impossible), and they normally engage in pleasant conversation and enjoy the food. However, an ordinary family meal is by definition not a markedly festive occasion, and it is not necessarily the product of the cooperation of many helpers. Large numbers of people are not present: nuclear families are not as big as they once were, and relatives do not necessarily live nearby.

Family food diaries kept by Breaux Bridge high school students for this study indicate that the dishes served at ordinary family meals are usually those described as Cajun. However, about one-fourth of the family meals described in the diaries consist of or include non-Cajun dishes, such as broiled sirloin steak; baked potatoes; macaroni, ham, and cheese casseroles; Mexican food (probably the favorite "ethnic" food in Acadiana); and convenience foods. Such dishes are rarely served at food events that are called Cajun, and they are not the focus of large-scale events resembling the special Cajun food-related events. A Cajun host does not often invite large numbers of people to watch him cook hamburgers or a pot of spaghetti and meatballs. Such foods are suitable for family meals or minor cookouts, but only *Cajun* foods are suitable for the special, large-scale, outdoor food events.

Not all special food events are viewed as Cajun food events. Although wedding receptions and club meetings include the serving of a complete Sunday-style dinner consisting of Cajun dishes, these occasions, along with holiday meals (other than Mardi Gras) and Sunday dinners, are not described as Cajun events. Although these events may affirm family, community, or organizational affiliations and identities, they do not usually celebrate *ethnic* identity through their activities. Cajun food is present, and Cajun sociability is in evidence, but Cajun environmental know-how is not clearly demonstrated, and outsiders are not usually present as a contrast group, except at some wedding receptions.

8.

Cajun Food and Ethnic Identity

Crawfish boils, boucheries and other special food events blend work and play, thus highlighting both Cajun competence and joie de vivre. In addition, at these events ethnic differences between Cajuns and outsiders are clearly evident and ethnic boundaries take on a special relevance.

Eating Ability and Ethnic Boundaries

Part of the power of the crawfish as an ethnic marker is derived from the fact that outsiders typically have difficulty in peeling and eating crawfish (see chapter 6). Outsiders, like very young Cajun children, cannot put food into their mouths because they lack the necessary mechanical skills. Two other Cajun foods require special mechanical skills on the part of diners. One is the boiled crab: separating the edible and inedible portions of boiled crabs is even more difficult and complex than peeling crawfish. Edible crabmeat is dispersed in shell-encased pockets throughout the crab's body and claws; it is not confined to a clearly demarcated tail area, as in the crawfish. Inedible internal portions of the crab are also dispersed throughout the body, rather than being confined largely to a relatively easily recognized and discarded "head." The diner must recognize and discard the crab's "face," "sandbags," "gills" (allegedly poisonous parts that resemble edible meat and are also called "dead man's fingers"), and various other internal organs with names known only to biologists. Because crab shells are very hard, the diner must possess a certain degree of physical strength (as well as a knife) to open and "pick" a crab. The role of an outsider as novice at a crab boil is similar to his or her role at a crawfish boil.

Boudin, too, can cause problems for novice eaters. Unlike most sausage casings, the skin of boudin is considered inedible, and it cannot easily be severed with the teeth. To avoid gagging on the leftover sausage casing of a partially eaten piece of boudin, a diner must push the sausage filling through the leftover casing, to the opening on its end. Some beginners fail to do this as they eat, and it is awkward and messy to do once the sausage has been half eaten. Newcomers receive explicit instructions on how to eat boudin. "Don't eat the skin," they are told. "It's like a tube of toothpaste. If you don't push from the bottom, you'll end up wasting it."

Unlike crawfish, crabs, and boudin, most Cajun foods do not require special mechanical skills on the part of the diner. Most cooked foods are served on plates or in bowls, and they are eaten with forks, spoons, and knives, as is typical of many foods eaten throughout the United States. Nonetheless, some outsiders have difficulty in eating various Cajun foods for reasons that are not related to mechanical skills. One such reason is physical, though culturally conditioned: some outsiders cannot tolerate the pepper content of many Cajun dishes, or the intense flavor of dark roast coffee. Another reason is cultural: certain Cajun foods violate the rules of edibility, or food taboos, held by some outsiders, especially middle-class, Anglo-American newcomers (see below). Being concerned about these factors does not mark an outsider as inept, but it does mark him or her as different from Cajuns.

Cajuns acknowledge that their food is very "hot," and they claim that a person must grow up eating this food in order to tolerate it physically. Outsiders virtually always characterize Cajun food as "hot," "spicy," or "full of pepper." Some outsiders see this as a positive trait, especially if they are accustomed to spicy foods because of their own upbringing, or if they have learned to enjoy peppery foods as adults. Other outsiders dislike Cajun food because of the pepper. They say that eating it is uncomfortable or painful, or that the rich seasonings make them ill, or that the cayenne pepper and other seasonings "ruin" the delicate flavor of some foods, particularly seafoods. An outsider's inability to eat highly seasoned foods marks him as different and provokes mild laughter or concern among locals. For example, Cajun onlookers found it humorous that the members of a visiting national theater group had difficulty tolerating the pepper content of the food routinely served to children at a Lafayette Parish elementary school cafeteria. Some male newcomers say that they have sometimes felt that they were being lightheartedly challenged to eat hot foods by Cajun male coworkers and friends. However, Cajuns more often express concern or sympathy for the plight of outsiders, or disappointment if they do not like the food. Many local people have said to me, "You don't have to force yourself to eat this if it's too hot," or have otherwise indicated sympathy or concern over the potential consequences of eating peppery foods. Several cooks have noted that they reduce the pepper content of food when diners are known to be "English-speakers," "Americans," "tourists," or "new people." The pepper content in the food of the tourist-oriented Cajun restaurants is considerably less than that of restaurants with a local clientele; it is also less than that of home-cooked food in the Breaux Bridge area.

THE REVERSAL OF FOOD TABOOS

Cajuns are aware that some outsiders categorize certain Cajun foodstuffs as inedible or repulsive. An elderly woman says, "When you tell people what's in our boudin or our hogshead cheese, it turns their sensitivity." A middle-aged man says, "A lot of these new people won't eat crawfish, or turtle, or garfish, or even squirrel. They're missing something good." Older people say that in the past, outsiders were more openly critical of Cajun food habits; they labeled Cajuns as people who "eat anything," or who "eat garbage." Today Cajun food is very popular with many outsiders, but some people still hold opinions similar to those of their earlier counterparts. For example, one Anglo-American from New Orleans says, "I like some Cajun foods, such as chicken gumbo and jambalaya, but I would never eat such a thing as boudin." A woman raised on various military bases throughout the world says, "Jambalaya and crawfish are great, while things like raw oysters are disgusting." Some outsiders openly criticize the activities that take place at certain Cajun food events. The Grand Boucherie des Cajuns in St. Martinville has provoked several newcomers to write letters to the editor of the local newspaper, complaining that hog butchering should not be put on public display. A friend of one of the writers explains her support of their sentiments:

> We had just moved to Lafayette from the East Coast. We read in the paper about the Boucherie in St. Martinville. They advertised it as a family event, so we decided to go and bring our five-year-old daughter. We really didn't know what a "boucherie" was—we didn't know that it was a hog-killing. When they stuck the knife in the pig's neck, it screamed for what seemed like five minutes. It was barbaric. I don't want my daughter exposed to things like that. I think they should ban the Boucherie, or they should at least be forced to advertise it for what it is—a savage custom.

Other outsiders occasionally criticize Mardi Gras chicken chasing on similar grounds.

Although it is difficult to generalize about the food habits and attitudes of a group as amorphous as "outsiders in Acadiana," several factors appear to motivate some outsiders (especially middle-class Americans) to avoid certain Cajun foods and food events. Some outsiders categorize some Cajun foods as inedible because they are derived from animals the outsiders categorize as inedible. The insectlike appearance and habitat of the crawfish moves some people to classify it as vermin. Louisiana market researchers seeking to create a market for nutria meat have said that "nobody wants to eat nutria because, at heart, nobody wants to eat a big, ugly, overgrown rat" (Baton Rouge *State Times*, January 18, 1982). Many Cajuns, it should be noted, feel the same way about nutria. Other animals viewed as inherently inedible by some outsiders include frogs, turtles, garfish, alligator, squirrel, opossum, raccoon, and muskrat. These animals are products of the local natural environment, and they are not likely to be familiar as food items to urbanized or suburbanized outsiders.[1] In fact, some Cajuns also do not eat opossum, raccoon, muskrat, or nutria, claiming that these foods are inedible or repulsive. Similar-

---

1. Of course, Cajuns are not the only people in the United States who eat the "controversial" foods discussed here. Many of these foods were important to the frontier diet throughout the American South and much of the United States (Taylor 1982:1–35), and some southerners continue to eat these foods. Southerners, too, have been ridiculed for similar violations of "American" middle-class norms. For example, the "aberrant" food habits of southern mountain dwellers are the basis of numerous jokes on "The Beverly Hillbillies" television series.

ly, some outsiders view certain parts of edible animals as inedible—pig or beef hearts, spleen, tripe, brains, stomach, or tongue. In addition, some outsiders are offended by the visible killing and dissection of animals at boucheries, Mardi Gras, and seafood boils.

These observations suggest that some people have a tendency to avoid as inedible or repulsive foods that are clearly derived from living animals, that are clearly "of nature." These include food made from wild animals that are rarely or never brought into the sphere of culture by being bred and cared for by humans; parts of farm animals that look like anatomically functioning organs; and food made from animals that look like animals even after they are cooked. Furthermore, these outsiders avoid food events at which the killing of animals (including those they may be accustomed to eat in other contexts) clearly demonstrates the natural source of human foods.

Most Cajuns, on the other hand, do not share these tendencies. Unlike more urbanized people, many Cajuns commonly derive some of their food directly from the environment. They are familiar with those preliminary food-processing steps, such as slaughtering, skinning, cleaning, and butchering, which are obscured from the view of people who always buy their more fully processed foods at grocery stores. From the Cajun point of view, this type of outsider appears squeamish or naive. For example, an anecdote commonly told in south Louisiana involves a tourist who yells for the waitress when he finds a crab claw in a bowl of gumbo. Another anecdote tells of a woman who feels sick after she learns that the "chicken" legs she has just enjoyed eating were actually frog legs. One Cajun small-town native who moved to Baton Rouge for industrial employment found that certain of his foodways offended his non-Cajun, city neighbors. An avid weekend hunter, he regularly returned to his Baton Rouge apartment with deer, squirrels, or wildfowl, which he skinned or plucked, cleaned, and cooked in the communal yard shared by other tenants. His neighbors asked him to stop this practice, telling him that they did not want to witness activities that, to them, were both repulsive and indicative of cruelty to animals. He refused their request, saying, "You cook hamburgers out here all the time. Where do you think that ground meat comes from?"

Some Cajuns have responded to criticism of their "repulsive" food habits by flaunting them as a positive rather than negative symbol. A common bumper sticker in Acadiana in the early 1980s proclaimed, "Coonasses [or Cajuns] make better lovers because they eat anything." Some people proudly claim that "a Cajun will eat anything that doesn't eat him first." The jokes and slogans that emphasize the less delicate aspects of crawfish eating also illustrate this point. A Cajun who was present when a California film crew was shooting a "documentary" film on Cajun life recounts this incident:

> The film crew approached a teenage girl and asked her, "What do Cajuns eat?" She replied, "Oh, we eat anything—'possum tails, alligator snouts, chicken feet—anything we can get, we eat." Of course, she doesn't eat these things. I doubt that her family eats 'possum stew, much less 'possum tails. She was teasing the film crew, and she was telling them what they wanted to hear. I'm not sure whether or not they knew that she was putting them on.

Cajuns occasionally emphasize the more "natural" aspects of their food-ways in actual food situations. One elderly Breaux Bridge man, known for his playful personality, made a point of helping me learn about the less conventional types of Cajun food. He repeatedly told me that I should eat some boiled turtle eggs, and for months he looked for wild turtles, promising to invite me for turtle eggs when he found some. When he finally caught a freshwater turtle, which was preparing to lay its eggs, he called me to meet him and some other locals for this old-time treat. He arrived with two paper bags, one containing the eggs and one containing the still-beating heart of the turtle. He placed the heart on a paper towel on the table in front of me and told me to watch it to see how long it would continue to beat. As the eggs were being boiled and eaten, he repeatedly directed my attention to the heart. Cajuns do not normally eat turtle eggs while watching the still-beating heart of the turtle. He had set up a situation in which the natural origins of a food were extremely clear, and he obviously enjoyed this test of an outsider's squeamishness. In addition, the eating of boiled turtle eggs is likely to present problems for some outsiders, even without the presence of the heart. A person whose experience with eggs is limited to chicken eggs will find that turtle eggs violate his or her conception of what an egg should be, and that they require a method of eating not associated with eating chicken eggs. Turtle eggs are small and round, with leathery shells. The white does not solidify when they are cooked, and the yolk is both sticky and gritty. To eat a turtle egg, a person must tear a hole in the leathery shell and suck the partially liquid contents from the shell. Thus, eating turtle eggs, like eating crawfish, demands intimacy between the diner and the food. Moreover, turtle eggs, like crawfish, retain their natural form after they are cooked.

Adherence to specific food taboos commonly marks an ethnic group as different from its neighbors (Douglas 1972:71–80; De Vos and Romanucci-Ross 1975:369; Simoons 1961:3) Do food taboos play a similar role in maintaining Cajun ethnic identity? Food taboos are relevant to Cajun identity not because Cajuns perceive themselves as maintaining them, but rather because they perceive themselves as violating other people's food taboos. They are different from outsiders partly because they eat certain foods that some outsiders categorize as inedible.

When outsiders first pointed out this difference to Cajuns, by criticizing their food habits, some Cajuns were ashamed or embarrassed. Like other formerly stigmatized aspects of Cajun culture, however, these food habits have undergone a reversal in value. Some Cajuns flaunt the fact that they violate other people's food taboos, that they "eat anything." Other Cajuns take a different approach, by touting these foods as gourmet or as part of a folk legacy (see below). Those outsiders who refuse to eat certain Cajun foods are, by contrast, both squeamish and foolish. Compared to environmentally competent Cajuns, who are comfortable with nature and with the natural aspects of foods, these outsiders are anxious and awkward when confronted with the natural aspects of foods and foodways. Furthermore, Cajuns can enjoy these foods and "have a good time" at associated food events, whereas the rules of edibility held by some outsiders cause them to "miss something good"—good food, good times, and good company. Thus Cajuns' self-perceived violation of other people's food taboos confirms Cajuns' stereotypes of outsiders, and it also indirectly affirms two themes of Cajun identity: environmental competence and sociability.

Although Cajuns sometimes joke that they "eat anything," and some Cajuns playfully flaunt this assertion, it is not true that Cajuns eat anything. Cajuns generally share the food taboos common to many western peoples. They do not eat insects, worms, cats, dogs, or algae, all of which are nutritious and readily available in their habitat. Unlike some of their continental French relatives, they consider horse meat to be inedible. Unlike their south Louisiana neighbors of Mediterranean descent, they do not eat octopus, which exists in local coastal waters. In the early 1980s some Cajuns in St. Martin Parish expressed revulsion at the alleged food habits of their new Vietnamese neighbors, who were rumored to eat cats, dogs, seagulls, shrimp heads, and rotten fish. The latter example clearly illustrates that Cajuns do hold food taboos, and that these are latent identity markers. We may suspect that if Cajuns were in frequent contact with large numbers of people whose foodways violated Cajun rules of edibility, then Cajun food taboos would be significant identity markers. But the Cajun social ecology contains far more people whose rules of edibility exclude certain Cajun foods. Therefore, the perceived violation by Cajuns of others' food taboos is more important to ethnic contrast and identity than is the maintenance of Cajuns' generally western food taboos.

FOODWAYS AND THE LOOSENING OF BOUNDARIES

Although Cajuns say that some outsiders find some Cajun foods to be repulsive, and although some outsiders cannot or will not eat intensely flavored foods or those that require special eating skills, Cajuns also strongly emphasize that most outsiders like Cajun food and admire Cajuns' culinary skills. Many outsiders, including the national media, confirm and encourage this belief among Cajuns. Cajun restaurants are extremely popular among tourists; local people cite Cajun food as one of the main factors that attract tourists to Acadiana. Lafayette city promoters claim that Lafayette has more restaurants per capita than any other city in the United States. The Louisiana State Office of Tourism promotes both Cajun and New Orleans "Creole" food in its pamphlets and nationally distributed newspaper and magazine advertisements designed to lure tourists to the state. National magazines and major newspapers occasionally carry articles about Cajun food, and virtually every popular article or book on Cajuns mentions their "famous" food. Food critic and journalist Calvin Trillin devoted a chapter of his book *American Fried* (1974) to Breaux Bridge, its festival, and its food. He appeared on "The Tonight Show" twice during my field work period, and both times he mentioned Breaux Bridge and Cajun food, much to the delight of Breaux Bridge natives. During the 1980s the national attention to Cajun food greatly increased, to the point of becoming a national fad among food critics, travel writers, and restaurant patrons (see below). The flattering attention given to Cajun cuisine by outsiders confirms Cajuns' assertions that their lifestyle is infectious or seductive—that outsiders will want to be like Cajuns once they have experienced the Cajun lifestyle.

Contemporary Cajuns socialize with newcomers to the region in many everyday situations (such as work or school) in which ethnicity is often irrelevant. Food events, however, offer an opportunity for Cajuns to interact with outsiders in a setting in which Cajun identity is both a relevant and a positive factor. Cajuns commonly invite outsiders to special Cajun food events. Because the guest list for one of these events is normally long, such an event provides an appropriate opportunity for a host to entertain acquaintances and friends of friends. Although Cajuns are temporarily socially distinguished as Cajuns at these events—they are the active providers of ethnically marked foods, and non-Cajun guests are the passive recipients—these events also provide an opportunity for Cajuns to easily *include* newcomers in their social sphere while simultaneously displaying their cultural distinctiveness. Thus, these food events help maintain symbolic boundaries, without necessitating the closure of social boundaries. This point is particularly important in light of the fact that Cajuns describe themselves as friendly and describe their lifestyle as attractive to others. By contrast, the speaking of French as an expression of ethnicity automatically prevents communication, and hence unhampered social interaction, between Cajuns and non-French-speaking outsiders. Most outsiders can enjoy some or all types of Cajun foods and food events, but monolingual English speakers, who constitute the majority of newcomers and tourists in Acadiana, cannot possibly participate in a French-language conversation.

As noted earlier, the cooking and eating of crawfish, as well as the physical nature of the food itself, suggest a theme of unity or intimacy between people and nature, between people and their food, and among people. Although this theme is most prominent at crawfish boils and crab boils, it can be detected at other food events as well. The presence of live animals at food events suggests intimacy between humans and nature, as does the lifelike form of some foods. Boiled crawfish, crabs, and shrimp are similar in appearance to their living counterparts. The crustacean shells used as containers for stuffed crabs and in crawfish bisque are also reminders of the living form of the animal these shells once contained. Raw oysters, if eaten immediately after they have been opened (the preferred way), are still alive when eaten. Eating food with one's hands, or placing inedible portions of food into one's mouth (as when sucking the head of a crawfish) also suggests a theme of unity or intimacy. Cajuns eat all boiled seafoods with their hands, and they commonly eat freshly opened raw oysters by sucking the oyster into their mouths directly from the open half-shell. Because many forms of gumbo contain crab pieces and claws or bony parts of chicken or game animals, diners must remove the inedible bones from the gravy with their hands, or pause to peel a sauce-covered crab claw.[2] People eat boudin with their hands, and some people eat the roast pork at a cochon de lait with their hands. At one "Coonass" cochon de lait (so termed by the host) that I attended, the guests served themselves the roast meat by pulling chunks of it from the whole hog with their hands.

At crawfish boils, the theme of intimacy or unity is reiterated through seating arrangements and the method of serving the food. Long communal tables and benches are commonly used at all outdoor Cajun food events. Boiled crabs and shrimp may be served in communal mounds, like crawfish, but most other foods are served on plates. A person's plate marks off "his" food and "his" place at the table. However, the size and location of individual places normally are not designated in advance by setting the table, and individuals are not directed to take specific, predetermined places at a table, through the use of place cards or precise verbal instructions. Exceptions to these rules would mark an event as extremely formal and highly unusual.

Cajuns do not exclude acquaintances (who may be non-Cajuns) from those events which most strongly suggest a theme of intimacy in various ways. In fact, the events that reflect an intensified unity or intimacy among in-group members are precisely those to which relatively distant acquaintances or new friends are most likely to be invited. This apparent paradox can be understood in light of Cajuns' belief that they can convert other people to the Cajun lifestyle by showing them how to relax and how to enjoy the good things in life, including food and festive companion-

---

2. The removal of bones from gumbo is not as problematical as peeling crawfish or eating boudin. However, some outsiders find this task distasteful and awkward, and they sometimes do not know where to put the bones. It is noteworthy that soup bowls with extra-wide rims are referred to as "gumbo bowls" in Louisiana. The rim provides the disposal site for the bones or crab shells.

ship. It would be inconsistent for Cajuns to exclude outsiders from the events that best illustrate Cajun esprit de corps and joie de vivre, or to withhold from outsiders the special foods that are believd to be part of the appeal or attractiveness of the Cajun lifestyle.

THE MEANING OF FOOD AT EVERYDAY MEALS

Food is not usually served in the context of special events that clearly affirm Cajun ethnicity. It is usually served at domestic meals, at which no outsiders are present as a contrast group, and where environmental skills and intensified sociability are not necessarily clearly evident or emphasized. Does food have any relevance to ethnicity in these everyday settings?

Anthropologist Mary Douglas suggests that all meals and dishes, regardless of whether they are part of a special occasion, carry the symbolic meanings inherent in the special food events. Within a given food system, there are regularities in the structuring of both meal patterns (course sequences, combinations of dishes served) and individual dishes (combination of ingredients according to dimensions such as solid/liquid, hot/cold, flavorful/bland). These regularities of physical and temporal structuring are fairly consistent, according to Douglas's analysis of British meals. "Meals are ordered in scale of importance and grandeur through the week and the year. The smallest, meanest meal metonymically figures the structure of the grandest, and each unit of the grand meal figures again the whole meal—or the meanest meal. The perspective created by these repetitive analogies invests the individual meal with additional meaning" (Douglas 1972:67). Food thus functions as an art form. As is the case with music and poetry, the repetition and transformation of structural characteristics gives the food system "all the mimetic and rhythmic qualities of other symbolic systems" (Douglas 1974:88, 1982:105–13).

The combination of a highly seasoned, long-cooked meat or seafood with rice forms the basis for many Cajun dishes, and for many Cajun meals as well. This pattern occurs at everyday family meals, and it is elaborated upon at Sunday dinners by the addition of side dishes. For very special community/family events, such as wedding receptions or church fund-raisers, the pattern is further developed: side dishes are added, and the major components are increased in number (two kinds of seasoned meats or seafoods, two kinds of rice). Of the special Cajun food events, only oyster openings and shrimp boils violate the basic meal structure, since the central item (plus beer) may be the only food served. Crawfish, crabs, and sometimes shrimp are boiled with large pieces of the usual seasoning vegetables, plus potatoes (instead of rice), so these dishes conform to the pattern. The typical Cajun snack—a piece of boudin—also recalls the basic structure of the meal and dish, since boudin is rice dressing in a sausage casing. In all cases, the temporal dimension of the meal (the sequencing of courses) is the same: all food is served at the same time, and preferably on the same plate (if there is enough room). Only desserts, which are often omitted from Cajun meals, conform to a rule of sequencing—they are served last.

Following Douglas's logic, we may conclude, for example, that a dish of gumbo served as a family supper carries the meaning of a dish of gumbo served at Mardi Gras or at another special food event. Furthermore, because gumbo follows the basic structure of dishes (and meal patterns) found at most special Cajun food events, an ordinary bowl of gumbo also carries all the meanings associated with these events, including the attention given to environmental skills and sociability, and to ethnic boundaries. Thus, any food that fits the structured aesthetic system has "mimetic" qualities, regardless of the context in which it is eaten. The eating of these foods expresses or recalls ethnicity in any setting. Consider this remark by a Breaux Bridge resident: "When I lived in Washington, I experienced a great desire for gumbo. I would call up my mother, and she would send me some, or I would fly home for some. I don't know if it was the dish itself, or all the times and people I associated with it. . . . "

FOOD: A PRAGMATIC SYMBOL

For a cultural pattern to function successfully as an ethnic symbol, it must be pragmatic—that is, it must be accessible, flexible, and compatible with nonethnic aspects of people's lives (Gans 1979:205). For contemporary Cajuns, food is a pragmatic symbol.

Cajun foods are accessible to virtually all Cajuns. Cajuns can purchase most traditional ingredients at retail stores. The majority of Cajuns have ready access to the local natural environment, and many people continue to acquire some of their foodstuffs through farming, gardening, hunting, trapping, and fishing. Even the animals that must be acquired directly from the wild are still fairly abundant, despite the ongoing destruction of their habitats. The farming of some wild animals (crawfish, catfish, alligators) further assures their ready availability to consumers, as do modern methods of preserving and distributing foodstuffs. It is significant that Cajuns can procure their traditional foodstuffs themselves (even though most do not do so on an everyday basis), and that they can acquire the traditional ingredients fresh, relatively unprocessed, or even alive from local stores. Because they can acquire relatively unprocessed ingredients, they are able to continue those processing activities (preliminary to cooking) that are so important to the symbolic power of their food.

Contemporary Cajuns also have ready access to the knowledge and skills required for producing dishes that conform to the traditional aesthetic. There has never been a widespread or wholesale abandonment of traditional food aesthetics by Cajuns; contemporary knowledge of traditional Cajun foodways is the result of an unbroken chain of tradition. Those older Cajuns who discouraged their children from learning to speak French still teach their children, their grandchildren, and their great-grandchildren how to roast pigs, peel crawfish, skin squirrels, plant vegetables, season gumbo, and brown flour for a roux.

Cajuns do not need an organization for the revival of ethnic cuisine to teach and encourage them to eat and publicly display their foods, nor do they need import stores to supply them with foodstuffs from a now distant homeland. Cajuns have not left their Louisiana homeland, and time and space do not separate them from their traditional cultural food patterns. In towns like Breaux Bridge, there is little need for "convenience" ethnic foods.

Cajun food is a flexible ethnic symbol, and it is acceptable as such to a wide variety of Cajuns. Like crawfish, other foods can be manipulated and interpreted to suit a refined style or an earthy style—or any number of styles. Gumbo is served from fine china tureens at formal dinner parties and from oversized cast-iron pots at rowdy festivals. A Lafayette restaurant that caters to a wealthy clientele has transformed boudin into a gourmet hors d'oeuvre by cutting it into bite-sized pieces, broiling it (rather than simmering or steaming it), and serving it on heated, cast-iron steak pans. The skin of this boudin is edible. Ordinary boudin, however, remains the favorite snack of bar patrons and working men. Some Cajuns interpret their consumption of less conventional foods, such as frogs, crawfish, or alligator, as an indicator of an earthy lifestyle: Cajuns "eat anything" and shock outsiders by doing so. Other Cajuns interpret their consumption of these same foods as an indication of refinement and sophistication: these are gourmet foods and offer no more cause for squeamishness than truffles, escargots, or caviar. Each group perceives itself as departing from "American" norms, but each group interprets this departure in terms consistent with its own ethnic style. Similarly, one St. Martin Parish resident describes his family boucherie as "a real Coonass party—lots of food, beer, and fun," while the elite town of St. Martinville advertises its boucherie as a presentation of the Cajun folk heritage and refers to it in the *French* language: it is called the Grand Boucherie des Cajuns. Restaurants that list *écrevisses* and *crevettes* on their menus—in the Genteel Acadian style—are likely to be more expensive than those that list crawfish and shrimp. Thus Cajuns of different ethnic styles tailor the preparation of Cajun food, within limits, and the context and mode in which the food is presented to suit their styles, and they interpret the meaning of a particular food or food event differently. However, in each case the food or food event is Cajun, and it distinguishes Cajuns from outsiders.

The procuring, cooking, and eating of Cajun foods do not interfere with other aspects of life, such as schooling or business. In fact, Cajun foodways are commonly enlisted as an aid in conducting business with other Cajuns and with outsiders to the region. One of Lafayette's legendary "illiterate Cajun millionaires," who made his fortune in the oil-field service industry, rents an apartment for use as his in-town camp and cooking site. Each weekend he cooks for clients and for all of his employees, from janitors to vice presidents. Cajun company managers or blue-collar workers often entertain their clients or coworkers by taking them hunting or fishing. Large and small corporations commonly hire Cajun cooks, sometimes from among the ranks of their employees, to cook boudin, crawfish, or gumbo for company parties and other special events. When a Japanese corporation ceremonially opened the "world's largest grain elevator" on the old "Acadian Coast" of the Mississippi River, local towns showed their gratitude for this boon to their economy by treating the Japanese executives to a Cajun-style jambalaya cookout and dance. College students earn money for campus organizations by hosting Cajun food events, and political candidates, both Cajun and non-Cajun, eat local specialties at political rallies in Acadiana.

EPILOGUE

During the 1980s, Cajun food became more famous than ever before, and also a bigger business. The mid-1980s interest in Cajun food was inspired partly by the 1984 New Orleans World's Fair, which drew tourists and journalists to exhibits on Cajun culture, and partly by the publication in 1984 of the cookbook, *Chef Paul Prudhomme's Louisiana Kitchen.*

Prudhomme, proprietor of the popular K-Paul's restaurant in New Orleans's French Quarter, is a native of Louisiana's southwestern prairie country who grew up cooking and eating traditional Cajun food. As an adult he became a trained chef and professional restaurateur, skilled in the presentation of food in a commercial setting with a broad clientele—a situation that requires that food be selected, cooked, and served to guests in ways quite different from home cooking. Prudhomme's nationwide marketing efforts have included best-selling cookbooks, his own line of seasoning powders, videotapes, personal appearances and cooking demonstrations, and guest spots on national television shows.

As a professional chef, Prudhomme created a dish called blackened redfish. He devised his blackening method of quickly cooking fish at very high temperatures in order to achieve the taste of fish cooked over a fire (Prudhomme et al. 1987:182). His blackening seasoning powder is also his own creation. Blackened redfish and other blackened meats and seafood have received a great deal of national media attention as Cajun dishes. However, blackened food was not known among the general population when field work for this study was done; Prudhomme first cooked blackened redfish in 1980 (see Prudhomme et al. 1987:182).

Blackened redfish and other blackened foods represent a new, creative variation on traditional Cajun cooking. Prudhomme drew upon his lifetime of experience with food and cooking in the folk setting, plus his skill as a professional chef, and elaborated upon these as a creative individual. Although it is a new dish, blackened redfish has traditional qualities. Blackening takes browning to the limit. The seasoning for this dish is peppery, and the basic ingredient (redfish) is a product of the Louisiana environment, a sport fish once associated primarily with the traditional dish called redfish courtbouillon. And, unless one owns a restaurant kitchen, blackened redfish is best prepared outdoors (like many special Cajun foods), where the heat and smoke can easily dissipate. In addition, as a cook and performer, Prudhomme reflects the tendency for Cajun men to enjoy the performance aspects of cooking.

Prudhomme's *Louisiana Kitchen* represents a haute cuisine variation on Cajun cooking. In a later book, *The Prudhomme Family Cookbook—Old-Time Louisiana Recipes* (1987) Prudhomme and his eleven brothers and sisters focused on the Cajun folk cooking of their family. The book is a thorough, insightful example of local people's description of their own culture. It is both a cookbook and an excellent description of traditional foodways, from procurement to eating, with a good bit of contextual information about food events and social relationships.

The national interest in Cajun food has led to growth in the food industry in Louisiana, including production and manufacturing. Since the early 1980s, the number of food manufacturers in Louisiana has tripled, partly because of the popularity of Cajun food and partly because of economic necessity in the depressed oil-based economy (Fonseca 1989:50). Some local companies make new versions of standard south Louisiana products, such as pepper sauces. Others have created new products referred to as Cajun, such as Zapp's potato chips, manufactured in Gramercy. Increased food manufacturing increases the need for fresh, locally produced ingredients derived from the Louisiana environment. Agriculture and aquaculture are growing and diversifying. For example, commercial vegetable harvests are increasing, and state officials are working to develop an alligator-hide-tanning industry in Louisiana as an off-shoot of the existing alligator meat business. (For an overview of Louisiana's expanding food industry, see Fonseca 1989:49–70.)

At the same time, out-of-state and national food manufacturing companies have started applying the term *Cajun* to their products, sometimes reducing Cajun food aesthetics to one dimension: very hot with pepper. Bob Odom, the state's commissioner of agriculture and forestry, says, "The only link some of these companies have with Acadiana is a call-forwarded WATS line. The poor-quality goods they label Cajun hurt our local processors and detract from the integrity of our native cuisine"

(Fonseca 1989:56). In response to this problem, the state has made available to Acadiana food producers a registered seal of authenticity that certifies a product as Cajun (Louisiana Department of Agriculture and Forestry 1991).

Fast-food retailers have also appropriated the word *Cajun* for their products, which include a "Cajun Whaler," a "Cajun McChicken" sandwich, a "New Orleans Cajun Pizza," and batter-dipped "Cajun" fried potatoes. These products are the creations of national chains and have little or no antecedents in traditional Cajun cuisine (see Ancelet n.d.).

Cajuns live in the modern world, which includes mass media and the mass marketplace. A 1988 article in *American Demographics*, which describes itself as "the magazine of consumer trends and lifestyles," stated that "the word 'Cajun' is shorthand for a rich culture whose music, folklore, and customs are still waiting to be discovered, packaged, and marketed" (Maines 1988:45). Both Cajuns and outsiders are taking part in this marketing process. The success of Cajun food and culture in the national media and marketplace affirms the value of Cajun ethnicity and the notion that Cajun culture is appealing to others—and also helps the local economy. At the same time, such success means that the word *Cajun* is being used and redefined in new contexts, sometimes by people who do not identify themselves as Cajuns or participate in Cajun life.

Cajun food is a marketable product, but it is much more than that. Cajun food is a source of meaning and value in the lives of a people, a medium that helps them express what it means to be Cajun.

Bibliography

Allain, Mathé. 1978. "Twentieth-Century Cajuns." In *The Cajuns: Essays on Their History and Culture*, pp. 129–41. Ed. Glenn Conrad. Lafayette: Center for Louisiana Studies, University of Southwestern Louisiana.

Ancelet, Barry J. 1983. "Courir du Mardi Gras." Oral presentation at the meeting of the Southern Anthropological Society, Baton Rouge.

Ancelet, Barry J. N.d. "Cultural Tourism in Cajun Country: Shotgun Wedding or Marriage Made in Heaven?" Unpublished Paper.

Ancelet, Barry J., Edwards, Jay, and Pitre, Glen. 1991. *Cajun Country*. Jackson: University Press of Mississippi.

Angers, Bob. 1979. "Anecdotes and Antidotes." *Acadiana Profile*, July/August, p. 13.

Angers, Trent. 1989. *The Truth about the Cajuns*. Lafayette, La.: Acadian House Publishing.

Barth, Fredrik, ed. 1969. *Ethnic Groups and Boundaries*. Boston: Little, Brown.

Bourg, Gene. 1985. "Cajun Rage May Die Before Real Food's Tasted." *The Times-Picayune/The States Item*, 17 December, D-12.

Bradshaw, James. 1977. "The Economic Impact of Oil and Gas on Louisiana." *Acadiana Profile*, July/August, pp. 25–68.

Brasseaux, Carl. 1987. *The Founding of New Acadia: The Beginnings of Acadian Life in Louisiana, 1765–1803*, Baton Rouge: Louisiana State University Press.

Broussard, Earlene. 1982. "Islands of the Marsh: An Interview with Artist Gerard Sellers." *Louisiane*, August, pp. 6–8.

Brown, Linda Keller, and Kay Mussell, eds. 1984. *Ethnic and Regional Foodways in the United States: The Performance of Group Identity*. Knoxville: University of Tennessee Press.

Carroll, James, and Blades, Holland C. 1974. *A Quantitative Analysis of the Amounts of South Louisiana Crawfish That Move to Market Through Selected*

Channels of Distribution. Department of Publications Research Series, no. 35. Lafayette: University of Southwestern Louisiana.

Chang, K. C. 1977. "Introduction." In *Food in Chinese Culture: Anthropological and Historical Perspectives*, pp. 3–21. Ed. K. C. Chang. New Haven: Yale University Press.

Comeaux, Malcolm. 1972. *Atchafalaya Swamp Life: Settlement and Folk Occupations*. Geoscience and Man Series, vol. 2. Baton Rouge: The School of Geoscience, Louisiana State University.

Conrad, Glenn. 1983. "The Acadians: Myths and Realities." In *The Cajuns: Essays on Their History and Culture*, pp. 1–18. 3rd ed. Ed. Glenn Conrad. Lafayette: Center for Louisiana Studies, University of Southwestern Louisiana.

Cutler, Blayne. 1989. "Is Cajun Hot or Not?" *American Demographics*, June, p. 16.

Davis, Edwin A. 1959. *Louisiana: The Pelican State*. Baton Rouge: Louisiana State University Press.

Del Sesto, Steven. 1975. "Cajun Social Institutions and Cultural Configurations." In *The Culture of Acadiana: Tradition and Change in South Louisiana*, pp. 121–42. Ed. Steven Del Sesto and Jon L. Gibson. Lafayette: University of Southwestern Louisiana.

De Vos, George, and Romanucci-Ross, Lola. 1975. "Ethnicity: Vessel of Meaning and Emblem of Contrast." In *Ethnic Identity: Cultural Continuities and Change*, pp. 363–90. Ed. George De Vos and Lola Romanucci-Ross. Palo Alto: Mayfield Publishing.

Dillemuth, C. H. 1974. "Louisiana Gumbo." Baton Rouge: The Katy-Did.

Dismukes, J. Philip. 1972. *The Center: A History of the Development of Lafayette, Louisiana*. Lafayette: City of Lafayette, La.

Ditchy, Jay K., ed. 1966. "Early Louisiana French Life: Folklore from the Anonymous Breaux Manuscript." Selected, arranged, and trans. George F. Reinecke. *Louisiana Folklore Miscellany* 2:1–58.

Dominguez, Virginia. 1977. "Social Classification of Creoles." *American Ethnologist* 4:589–602.

Dorman, James H. 1983. *The People Called Cajuns: An Introduction to an Ethnohistory*. Lafayette: The Center for Louisiana Studies, University of Southwestern Louisiana.

Douglas, Mary. 1972. "Deciphering a Meal." *Daedalus* 101:61–81.

Douglas, Mary. 1974. "Food as Art Form." *Studio International* 188:83–88.

Douglas, Mary. 1982. *In the Active Voice*. London: Routledge and Kegan Paul.

Edler, Tim. 1979. *The Adventures of Crawfish-Man*. Baton Rouge: Little Cajun Books.

Edler, Tim. 1980. *Crawfish-Man Rescues Ron Guidry*. Baton Rouge: Little Cajun Books.

Edmunds, James. 1981. "Lafayette: Prosperous and Proud." *Louisiana Life*, July/August, pp. 18–32.

Esman, Marjorie R. 1981. "The Celebration of Cajun Identity: Ethnic Unity and the Crawfish Festival." Ph.D. dissertation, Tulane University.

Farb, Peter, and Armelagos, George. 1980. *Consuming Passions: The Anthropology of Eating*. Boston: Houghton Mifflin.

Fiebleman, Peter S. 1971. *American Cooking: Creole and Acadian*. New York: Time-Life Books.

Fonseca, Mary, 1989. "Louisiana Food Processing—Recipe for Expansion." *Louisiana Life*, September/October, pp. 49–70.

Fontenot, Sharon M. 1967. "Food Customs in a Louisiana French Parish." M.A. thesis, Louisiana State University.

Fournet, Estelle M. 1939. "A Comparison of Food Habits in Non-French and French Louisiana. M.A. thesis, Louisiana State University.

Gans, Herbert J. 1979. "Symbolic Ethnicity: The Future of Ethnic Groups and Cultures in America." In *On the Making of Americans: Essays in Honor of David Riesman*, pp. 193–220. Ed. Herbert Gans, Nathan Glazer, Joseph Gusfield, and Christopher Jencks. Philadelphia: University of Pennsylvania Press.

Gillespie, Angus K. 1979. "Toward a Method for the Study of Food in American Culture." *Journal of American Culture* 2:393–406.

Gilmore, Harlan W. 1933. "Social Isolation of the French Speaking People of Rural Louisiana." *Social Forces* 12:78–84.

Ginn, Mildred K. 1940. "A History of Rice Production in Louisiana to 1896." *Louisiana Historical Quarterly* 23:3–47.

Greene, Johnny. 1986. "Why John Volz Couldn't Nail Edwin Edwards." *Southern Magazine*, October, pp. 48–80.

Gueymard, Ernest. 1973. "Louisiana's Creole-Acadian Cuisine." *Louisiana Review* 2:8–19.

Guirard, Greg. 1989. *Cajun Families of the Atchafalaya: Their Ways and Words*. Privately printed.

Guirard, Leona M. 1973. "Talk about Crawfish." Printed souvenir.

Gutierrez, C. Paige. 1984. "The Social and Symbolic Uses of Ethnic/Regional Foodways: Cajuns and Crawfish in South Louisiana." In *Ethnic and Regional Foodways in the United States: The Performance of Group Identity*, pp. 169–

182. Ed. Linda Keller Brown and Kay Mussell. Knoxville: University of Tennessee Press.

Gutierrez, C. Paige. 1985. "Louisiana Traditional Foodways." In *Louisiana Folklife: A Guide to the State*, pp. 150–159. Ed. Nicholas R. Spitzer. Baton Rouge: Louisiana Folklife Program, Office of Cultural Development, Department of Culture, Recreation, and Tourism.

Hallowell, Christopher. 1979. *People of the Bayou*. New York: E. P. Dutton.

Hill, Carole E. 1977. "Anthropological Studies in the American South: Review and Directions." *Current Anthropology* 18:309–26.

Hilliard, Sam B. 1972. *Hog Meat and Hoecake: Food Supply in the Old South, 1840–1860*. Carbondale: Southern Illinois University Press.

Huner, Jay V. 1990. "The Louisiana Crawfish Story." *Food Distribution Magazine*, February.

Huner, Jay V. 1991. "Crawfish Farming in Louisiana" (special fact sheet). Lafayette: Crawfish Research Center, University of Southwestern Louisiana, April.

Huner, Jay V., and Romaire, Robert P. 1990. "Crawfish Culture in the Southeastern U.S.A." *World Aquaculture*, December, pp. 58–65.

Jacobi, Herman J. 1937. *The Catholic Family in Rural Louisiana*. Washington, D.C.: The Catholic University of America Press.

Kammer, Edward J. 1941. *A Socio-economic Survey of the Marshdwellers of Four Southeastern Louisiana Parishes*. Washington, D.C.: The Catholic University of America Press.

Kane, Harnett T. 1943. *The Bayous of Louisiana*. New York: Bonanza.

Kane, Harnett T. 1944. *Deep Delta Country*. New York: Duell, Sloan, and Pearce.

Kane, Harnett T. 1949. *Queen New Orleans*. New York: William Morrow.

Lang, John S. 1978. "In Cajun Land, a Return to French Roots." *U.S. News and World Report*, May 15, pp. 31–32.

Leach, Edmund. 1970. *Claude Levi-Strauss*. New York: Viking Press.

Leach, Edmund. 1976. *Culture and Communication: The Logic by Which Symbols Are Connected*. Cambridge: Cambridge University Press.

Lee, Chan. 1960. "A Culture History of Rice with Special Reference to Louisiana." Ph.D. dissertation, Louisiana State University.

Le Page Du Pratz, Antoine Simon. 1774. *History of Louisiana*. London: T. Becket.

Lockett, Samuel H. 1969. *Louisiana as It Is: A Geographical and Topographical Description of the State*. Ed. Lauren C. Post. Baton Rouge: Louisiana State University Press.

Lomax, Alan. 1977. "Appeal for Cultural Equity." *Journal of Communication* 27:125–38.

Louisiana Crawfish Promotion and Research Board. 1991. "The Crawfish Are Coming." Press release. Baton Rouge: Louisiana Crawfish Promotion and Research Board.

Louisiana Department of Agriculture and Forestry. 1991. "Agriculture and Forestry Today with Commissioner Bob Odom." Press release. Baton Rouge: Louisiana Department of Agriculture and Forestry.

Louisiana Seafood Promotion and Marketing Board. N.d. "Crawfish" (fact sheet). Baton Rouge: Louisiana Seafood Promotion and Marketing Board.

McSherry, Julia M. 1982. "Crawfish: From Pond to Pot." *Louisiana Conservationist*, March/April, pp. 4–9.

Maines, John. 1988. "The Road to Mamou." *American Demographics*, May, pp. 45–47.

Mitcham, Howard. 1978. *Creole Gumbo and All That Jazz*. Reading, Mass. Addison-Wesley.

Moody, Michael W. 1980. *Louisiana Seafood Delight—The Crawfish*. Baton Rouge: Cooperative Extension Service, Louisiana State University.

Morgan, Bruce C. 1982. "The Night Has 1,000 Eyes." *Louisiana Life*, September/October, pp. 82–87.

Peacock, James L. 1975. *Consciousness and Change: Symbolic Anthropology in Evolutionary Perspective*. New York: John Wiley and Sons.

Perales, André-Paul. 1982. *Fanfou dans les bayous*. Gretna, La.: Pelican Publishing.

Pittman, Philip. 1973. *The Present State of the European Settlements on the Mississippi: 1770*. Facs. reprod. of 1770 ed. Gainesville: University of Florida Press.

Post, Lauren C. 1962. *Cajun Sketches from the Prairies of Southwest Louisiana*. Baton Rouge: Louisiana State University Press.

Prudhomme, Paul. 1984. *Chef Paul Prudhomme's Louisiana Kitchen*. New York: William Morrow.

Prudhomme, Paul, et al. 1987. *The Prudhomme Family Cookbook: Old-time Louisiana Recipes by the Eleven Prudhomme Brothers and Sisters and Chef Paul Prudhomme*. New York: William Morrow.

Reed, Revon. 1976. *Lache pas la patate*. Montreal: Editions Parti Pris.

Rees, Grover. 1976. *A Narrative History of Breaux Bridge*. St. Martinville, La.: Attakapas Historical Association.

Rickels, Patricia. 1983. "The Folklore of the Acadians." In *The Cajuns: Essays on Their History and Culture*, pp. 219–32. 3rd ed. Ed. Glenn Conrad. Lafayette: Center for Louisiana Studies, University of Southwestern Louisiana.

Robin C. C. 1966. *Voyage to Louisiana, 1803–1805*. Trans. Stuart O. Landry, Jr. New Orleans: Pelican Publishing. Orig. pub. Paris: F. Buisson, 1807.

Rushton, William F. 1979. *The Cajuns: From Acadia to Louisiana*. New York: Farrar, Straus and Giroux.

Saxon, Lyle, Dreyer, Edward, and Tallant, Robert, eds. 1945. *Gumbo Ya-Ya: A Collection of Louisiana Folk Tales*. New York: Bonanza.

Schweid, Richard. 1989. *Hot Peppers: Cajuns and Capsicum in New Iberia, Louisiana*. Berkeley: Ten Speed Press.

Simoons, Frederick J. 1961. *Eat Not This Flesh: Food Avoidances in the Old World*. Madison: University of Wisconsin Press.

Smith, T. Lynn, and Parenton, Vernon J. 1938. "Acculturation among the Louisiana French." *American Journal of Sociology* 44:355–64.

Smith, T. Lynn, and Post, Lauren C. 1937. "The Country Butchery: A Cooperative Social Institution." *Rural Sociology* 2:335–37.

Spitzer, Nicholas R. 1986. *Zydeco and Mardi Gras: Creole Identity and Performance Genres in Rural French Louisiana*. Ph.D. dissertation, University of Texas.

Steelman, Virginia P. 1974. *The Cultural Context of Food: A Study of Food Habits and Their Social Significance in Selected Areas of Louisiana*. Agricultural Experiment Station Bulletin 681. Baton Rouge: Center for Agricultural Sciences and Rural Development, Louisiana State University.

Surrey, N. M. Miller. 1916. *The Commerce of Louisiana During the French Regime, 1699–1763*. New York: Columbia University Press.

Taylor, Joe Gray. 1982. *Eating, Drinking and Visiting in the Old South: An Informal History*. Baton Rouge: Louisiana State University Press.

Tentchoff, Dorice. 1975. "Cajun French and French Creole: Their Speakers and the Questions of Identities." In *The Culture of Acadiana: Tradition and Change in South Louisiana*, pp. 87–109. Lafayette: University of Southwestern Louisiana.

Thwaite, Reuben Gold, ed. 1907. "Cuming's Tour to the West, 1807–1809. In *Early Western Travels, 1748–1846*, vol. 4, p. 339. New York: AMS Press. Rpt. of 1907 ed.

Trillin, Calvin, 1974. *American Fried*. New York: Doubleday.

Turner, Victor. 1969. "Forms of Symbolic Action: Introduction." In *Proceedings of the 1969 Annual Spring Meeting of the American Ethnological Society*, pp. 3–25. Ed. Robert F. Spencer. Seattle: University of Washington Press.

Warner, Charles Dudley. 1889. *Studies in the South and West.* New York: Harper and Brothers.

Whitfield, Irene T. 1939. *Louisiana French Folk Songs.* New York: Dover.

Woodward, C. Vann. 1960. *The Burden of Southern History.* Baton Rouge: Louisiana State University Press.

Index